C000182510

ALLEN BREED SERIES

The Allen Breed Series examines horse and pony breeds from all over the world, using a broad interpretation of what a breed is: whether created by the environment where it originally developed, or by man for a particular purpose, selected for its useful characteristics, or for its appearance, such as colour. It includes all members of the horse family, and breeds with closed or protected stud books as well as breeds and types still developing.

Each book in the Allen Breed Series examines the history and development of the breed, its characteristics and use, and its current position in Britain, together with an overview of the breed in America and worldwide. More difficult issues are also tackled, such as particular problems associated with the breed, and such controversies as the effect of the show ring on working breeds. The breed societies and their role in modern breeding policies are discussed.

BOOKS IN THE SERIES

The Appaloosa
The Arabian Horse
The Coloured Horse and Pony
The Fell Pony
The Hackney
The Haflinger
The Hanoverian
The Irish Draught Horse
The Morgan Horse
The Mule
The Quarter Horse
The Trakehner
The Welsh Mountain Pony

ALLEN BREED SERIES

The Shetland Pony

Riccalton Smuggler (rider: Nicky Rhodes) and Riccalton Trampas (rider: Lyndsay Wightman) at the Royal Windsor Horse Show 1994. (Photo by Hamish Mitchell.)

ALLEN BREED SERIES

The Shetland Pony

Anna Hodson

J. A. Allen

London

British Library cataloguing in publication data
A catalogue record for this book is available from the British Library

ISBN 0 85131 667 0

Published in Great Britain in 1997 by
J. A. Allen & Company Limited
1 Lower Grosvenor Place
London SW1W 0EL

© Anna Hodson 1997

Much of the material in this book has appeared before in a book by the same author, published by Crowood Press.

No part of this book may be reproduced or transmitted in any way or by any means, electronic or mechanical, including photocopy, recording, or any information storage and retrieval system, without permission in writing from the publishers. All rights reserved.

Series editor Elizabeth O'Beirne-Ranelagh
Text editor Susan Beer
Book production Bill Ireson
Printed in Hong Kong

Contents

Front cover: Ideal grazing conditions for Shetland ponies: Mrs D. W. Edwards's youngstock on the hills of Cumbria.

Endpapers
Front: Miss Jo Halnan driving Eastlands Slip Anchor (leader) and Meonwara Marble (wheeler) in tandem. *Back*: Tanygroes Tiree and Riccalton Trampas.

Acknowledgements

Many people have helped me with information and discussions. They are too many to name individually, except that I am glad to mention particularly the help given by Miss Grace Crook, until recently Secretary of the Shetland Pony Stud-Book Society, and by Derek and Joan O'Brien.

The following have very kindly lent me photographs of their ponies: the late Mrs C. Berry, Dr D. Bird, Mrs E. Braithwaite, Mrs J. Carter, the Duchess of Devonshire, Mrs D. W. Edwards, the late Mrs E. Hall, Miss J. Halnan, Mrs V. Hampton, Mrs S. Helps, Mrs E. House, Mrs D. W. J. O'Brien, Mesdames J. A. and J. R. Stevenson, Mrs A. Swinscow, Mr and Mrs P. J. Tindale, Mrs M. Tupper, Mrs R. G. Turvill, Mrs R. Webb and the Woods family.

My thanks also go to my husband, Robin Mann, who took a number of photographs for the book, and who asked so many good questions.

Introduction

In the very first volume of the Shetland Pony Stud Book is a formal description:

> The Shetland pony is often very handsome, with a small head, intelligent coun-
> tenance, short neck, fine towards the throttle, back short, quarters expanded, and
> powerful, legs flat and fine, and pretty round feet; ribs well laid on until within
> two inches of the hip bone, having great width and depth near the heart and
> lungs, shoulders well sloped, fore-arm and thighs strong and muscular. The
> height of carefully-bred ponies from selected parents when full-grown will gen-
> erally range from 9 to 10 hands.

Just a century later, the first-ever meeting of the Shetland Pony European
Committee (held at Edinburgh in August 1990) unanimously approved a new breed
standard:

Height
Registered stock must not exceed 40 inches (1.02 m) at three years or under, nor 42
inches (1.07 m) at four years old and over. Ponies are measured from the withers to
the ground, by measuring stick and a level stance, preferably concrete, should be
used.

Colour
Shetland ponies may be any colour known in horses, except spotted.

Coat
The coat changes according to the seasons of the year. A double coat in winter with
guard hairs which shed the rain and keep the pony's skin completely dry in the worst
of weather. By contrast, the summer coat is short and should carry a beautiful silky
sheen. At all times the mane and tail hair should be long, straight and profuse and the
feathering of the fetlocks straight and silky.

Head
The head should be small, carried well and in proportion. Ears should be small and
erect, wide set, but pointing well forward. Forehead should be broad with bold, dark,

intelligent eyes. Blue eyes are not acceptable. Muzzle must be broad with nostrils wide and open. Teeth and jaw must be correct.

Body
The neck should be properly set onto the shoulder which in turn should be sloping, not upright and end in a well-defined wither. The body should be strong, with plenty of heart room, well sprung ribs, the loin strong and muscular. The quarters should be broad and long with the tail set well up on them.

Fore legs
Should be well placed, sufficient good flat bone. Strong forearm. Short balanced cannon bone. Springy pasterns.

Hind legs
The thighs should be strong and muscular, with well shaped strong hocks, neither

An example of a Shetland pony absolutely true to the official breed standard: Hose Elan as a yearling filly (foaled 1991), owned and bred by Mesdames J. A. and J. R. Stevenson.

hooky nor too straight. When viewed from behind, the hind legs should not be set too wide apart nor should the hocks be turned in.

Feet
Tough, round and well shaped – not short, narrow, contracted or thin.

Action
Straight free action using every joint, tracking up well.

General
A most salient and essential feature of the Shetland Pony is its general air of vitality (presence), stamina and robustness.

A fine creature indeed. The Shetland is the most distinguished of all the native ponies. Everybody can recognise a Sheltie, not just by its small size, but by its especially attractive character. Thelwell struck a true note when he drew his cartoons of the Shetland as 'the' pony. Yet no other pure-bred pony can be so variable: a Shetland can be as tall as 42 inches (the height is always stated in inches, not hands and inches as for other breeds) or as small as 27 inches at maturity, a difference of 15 inches. Or to put it another way, the largest Shetlands are more than 50 per cent taller than the smallest ones. Shetland ponies come in a greater variety of colours than any other breed, though for many fans the classic black remains the ideal.

The Shetland pony's woolly winter coat is its greatest trademark, much needed in its native islands (where there is an average of 69 days of snow or sleet each winter) and still grown even in comfortable England or indeed in the tropics. The double coat, with hairs 6 inches long or more, so muffles the outline of the pony that you can hardly see that it is a pony at all: 'Little shagged animals, more resembling wild bears than any thing of the horse tribe', is how Sir Walter Scott described them. But in the summer Shetland ponies are as sleek as racehorses. Sometimes it is hard to believe that the shining mares can be the mothers of the fluffballs-on-stilts that follow them.

Shetlands have another characteristic which is not so widely known but which forms a large part of their charm for the people who love them: their long life. It is not at all unusual for a Shetland to live to thirty years, and even forty is no great age to them. Dr and Mrs Douglas, authors of the first book about Shetland ponies, made a touching comment: 'Everyone who really associates with them knows how disastrously short a time dogs and horses live: on no reasonable calculation can they grow

A Shetland in his ripe old age: Silver of Thorne, for many years the senior stallion at Mr and Mrs R. G. Turvill's Highwood Stud, enjoying the winter weather at the age of thirty-four. (His younger self can be seen in chapter 5.)

old with their owners. Even the Shetland pony fails of this, but he makes the bravest of attempts.'

No one should suppose that just because Shetland ponies are small and pretty they are simply toys. The late Major Maurice Cox, a great breeder and author of the standard work on Shetlands, was determined that 'We must keep the breed as useful as possible and not a purely ornamental one.' Their exceptional intelligence means that they can be trained to any job. A Shetland is the obvious choice for a child's first pony, not only because of its small size but also because of its generous temperament. Other advantages are its tough constitution and its unerring surefootedness. As for driving, Shetlands have a brilliant natural talent for the work, being full of courage, stamina and strength (Shetlands are easily the strongest equines in the world, in proportion to their size). The special attraction of the Shetland pony has never been better described than by the Douglases:

> He provides . . . the dual charm of a creature at once wild and tame – wild in his strong instincts, his hardihood, and his independence – domestic in his wisdom and sweet temper, his friendly confidence in mankind, and his subtle powers of ingratiation.

'A creature at once wild and tame': Lockinge Martin, bred by Mrs Guy Knight and owned by Mr and Mrs P. J. Tindale.

1 Early history

The Shetland pony is not only one of the most distinguished of the many varieties of the horse but is also probably one of the oldest. Zoologists generally agree that the true horse (or pony) *Equus caballus* originated in the plains of North America at the end of the Pliocene age, about two million years ago. A hugely successful species, it spread in all directions, and crossed over to Asia by the land bridge which then existed where now the Bering Strait separates Alaska from Siberia. These early horses colonised the Old World in three waves of migration: the first went southwards and were eventually domesticated by the herdsmen of Mongolia and the ancient civilisations of China; the second – and the most important from our present point of view – went straight across the steppes of Asia into the forests of Europe; and the third went south-west over the Caucasus mountains into Arabia and North Africa, to become the ancestors of the present-day Arab horse (and also of the Thoroughbred).

The prehistoric ponies of Europe

The early European pony was a cobby type of 12 or 13 hands high. The heavily forested landscape did not favour a larger animal, and the temperatures, appreciably colder than at present, called for a thick protective coat. These characteristics can be seen in the prehistoric rock paintings of Europe, which indicate that ponies were very numerous, and that they were hunted for meat.

These cobby ponies were very widespread, ranging right across Europe from Spain to Scandinavia. Confusingly, they are referred to in the zoological literature as 'Celtic' ponies; but these ponies have no connection with the Celtic peoples or culture, being far more ancient and widespread. They were certainly the ancestors of the Shetland pony; but unfortunately there is no firm evidence as to when they first reached the islands.

The smallest ponies

The process by which the prehistoric 'Celtic' pony evolved into the much smaller true Shetland must have been twofold.

Firstly, there is the general tendency for animals that live in cold climates to be both smaller and more compactly built than their relatives elsewhere. This arises from the need to conserve body heat in winter; it is best for the animal to have the

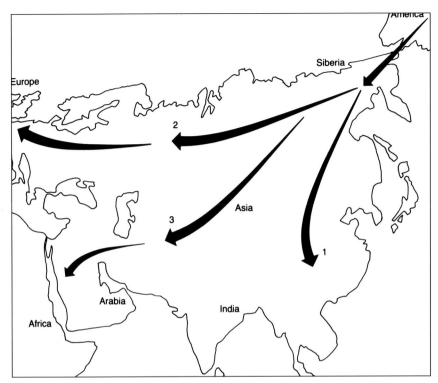

The migration of horses from America into Asia and Europe

smallest possible surface area in relation to its body size, that is, to have shorter limbs, a short back, thick neck, small ears, and so on. This tendency (known technically as Allen's Rule) can be seen in many animals (for instance the desert versus the arctic fox). All the northern races of ponies – Norwegian, Iceland, etc. – show it, but none to so marked a degree as the Shetland.

Secondly, in populations living on small islands natural selection tends to result in smaller animals. This is because the restriction of the island habitat means that there is a limited range that the animals can forage in. When food is short (as it is every winter on the Shetland Islands), animals that can get by with little to eat are more likely to survive. Larger animals will tend to die off, leaving the smaller survivors to breed the following year. Thus the population will come to consist entirely of animals that carry the gene (or genes) for smallness. It is not so much the

Allen's Rule: the extremities get smaller in animals that live in colder climates. (After Ernst Mayr, *Evolution and the Diversity of Life.*)

harshness of the climate that matters, it is the rationing of food imposed by the island habitat. The Norwegian and Icelandic breeds have to contend with equally hard winters, but because they are able to range more widely in search of food they have not been so severely selected for small size, and are therefore a hand or two taller. (However, there is a race of Norwegian ponies living on the island of Bodo which has become as small as the Shetland type, and for the same reason.)

It is also important to realise that the smallness of Shetland ponies is not due to a direct stunting through a lack of food while they are growing, it is solely the result of the ruthless action of natural selection in weeding out the genetically larger ponies. When Shetland ponies were first bred in England in the nineteenth century it was believed that they would grow much larger, and there was much puzzlement when such turned out not to be the case.

The first ponies on the Shetland Islands

Archaeologists do not think it likely that Shetland ponies first arrived on the islands by their own efforts. There was a time during the last Ice Age when the North Sea was still land, but the Shetland Islands are so far north that it would probably have been too cold at that time for wild ponies to survive there. More probably the ponies were brought to the islands later by the first settlers, along with their other livestock.

The first evidence of their presence comes from the late Bronze Age settlement at Jarlshof, near Sumburgh, dated to about 2,500 years ago. These ponies were of the same size as present-day Shetlands. It is not clear whether they were domesticated or not; their bones are found scattered about, and it is possible that they were simply being hunted for food.

The earliest signs of ponies being used in the Shetlands come from the time of the Viking invasion, in the early ninth century AD. The Vikings evidently brought with them their own ponies, which archaeologists have described as 'not of large size, but exceeding the very small breeds on Shetland today'. Nearly all the bones found were from adult ponies, which probably indicates that the Vikings brought over only strong ponies fit for war and work, and did not reckon to breed any ponies in such a remote colony.

The very fine sculptured stone known as the Bressay Stone, excavated near the

The Bressay Stone. It is about a thousand years old and shows a pony that may be a Shetland.

9

ruins of a very early church on the island of Bressay, opposite Lerwick, dates from about a century later. It shows a priest or monk riding a pony, but unfortunately one cannot deduce what size of pony it was, given the non-realistic artistic conventions of the time. This may be our first representation of a true Shetland pony, or it may only be a Viking one.

The Shetland pony in historical times

After the Viking period, there is no mention of Shetland ponies until the seventeenth century. Then nearly every visitor to the Islands began to remark on their virtues. The earliest account is by Captain John Smith, who spent a year on the Islands in 1633: 'Their Horses, which they call Shelties, some of which I have seen, are little bigger than Asses, but very durable.' At about the same time, Robert Monteith, an Orkney land-owner, visited friends in Shetland and wrote about the ponies:

> The Horses are most of them of a very small Size, not exceeding nine hand-breadth high; an Horse of twelve hand-breadth hight (which is but even rare here) is esteemed a very tall Horse, the least of the Horses here are sharp and full of metle above belief, they will carrie a Man and a Woman twenty miles a day, and will live till they be 30 or 40 years old, though they never are put in a Stable Summer or Winter, and are not allowed Shoes or Provender, but shift for themselves in the open fields.

A fine description of Shetland ponies came half a century later from John Brand, a minister sent to the Islands in 1700 by the General Assembly 'to visit and order the Churches there'. Whatever impression he formed of the brethren, he admired the ponies:

> They have a sort of little Horses called *Shelties*, then which no other are to be had, if not brought hither from other places, they are of less Size than the *Orkney* Horses, for some will be but 9 others 10 nives or Handbreadths high, and they will be thought big Horses there if eleven, and although so small yet they are full of vigour and life, and some not so high as others often prove to be the strongest, yea there are some, whom, an able Man can lift up in his arms, yet will they carry him and a Woman behind him 8 miles forward and as many back: Summer or Winter they never come into an House, but run upon the mountains in some places in flocks, and if at any time in Winter the storm be so great, that they are

straitened, for food, they will come down from the Hills, when the Ebb is in the sea, and eat the Sea-ware (as likewise do the Sheep), which Winter storme and scarcity of fodder puts them out of Case, and bringeth them so very low, that they recover not their strength till about St. John's Mass Day, the 24th. of June when they are at their best: They will live to a considerable age, as 26, 28, or 30 years, and they will be good riding Horses in 24 especially they'le be the more vigorous and live the longer, if they be 4 Years old before they be put to Work. These of a black Colour are Judged the most durable, and the pyeds often prove not so good; they have been more numerous than they are now; the best of them are to be had in *Sanston* and *Eston*, also they are good in *Waes* and *Yell*, these of the least size are in the Northern Isles of *Yell* and *Unst*.

The Coldness of the Air, the Barrenness of the Mountains on which they feed, and their hard usage may occasion them to keep so little, for if bigger Horses be brought into the Countrey, their kind within a little time will degenerate; And indeed in the present case, we may see the Wisdome of Providence, for, their way being deep and Mossie in Many places, these lighter Horses come through, when the greater and heavier would sink down: and they leap over ditches very nimbly, yea up and down rugged Mossy braes or hillocks with heavy riders upon them, which I could not look upon but with Admiration, yea, I have seen them climb up braes upon their knees, when otherwise they could not get the height overcome.

The Shetland pony – a pure breed?

The Shetland pony, unique and unmistakable, has been remarkably resistant to outside influence, having been apparently unchanged since the time of the Bronze Age. However, there have been many non-native equine arrivals in the Islands, and some authorities have claimed to be able to discern two distinct types among pure-bred Shetlands, which reflect the legacy of these later arrivals.

Arab-type horses

The horses used by the Roman army were bred by crossing European Celtic-type ponies with the taller faster horses of Arabian type that the Romans had found in the eastern parts of their empire. The resulting animals were 13 hands high or a bit over; their remains have been found in Britain, as far north as Hadrian's Wall. There is some possibility, though very remote, that descendants of these Roman cavalry horses spread among the native ponies of Scotland and eventually got as far north as Shetland.

The earliest feasible direct contact with horses of Arabian blood occurred in the twelfth century, when the Crusaders who went to Palestine encountered the impressive swift horses of the Saracens. It is recorded in the Orkneyinga Saga that Earl Rognvald of Orkney came home from the Crusade on horseback as far as Denmark, then by ship to Norway and thence home. Perhaps Rognvald and his companions brought the same eastern horses with them all the way from the Holy Land to the Orkneys and Shetlands.

A myth persists that Spanish horses came ashore when the *Gran Grifon*, one of the flagships of the Spanish Armada, was wrecked on Fair Isle in 1588. Even if the animals did manage to get onto the land (which would have been difficult on such a rocky coast and in stormy weather), it would not be at all likely that a highly bred Spanish horse would be able to survive the conditions on the islands. But they could perhaps have left a few descendants; one should not too hastily dismiss the stories that are found in folk mythology.

Norway

Throughout the Middle Ages Shetland's main contact was with Norway, under whose crown the islands remained until 1468 when they were pledged to James III of Scotland as part of the dowry of Margaret, Princess of Norway. There may well have been some importing of ponies from Norway to Shetland during those centuries, particularly if the Norsemen wanted to use larger ponies than those native to the islands, but the impact on the Shetland pony type would have been negligible as they were already drawn from the same prehistoric ancestral stock as the Norwegian ponies.

Iceland

Shetland tradition has it that the white markings on piebalds and skewbalds derive from imported Icelandic ponies. Icelanders and Shetlanders have always been on neighbourly terms, and both were part of the Norwegian kingdom for a long time, so it is quite likely that ponies were taken from one place to the other. As for the white markings, they are caused by a single gene, and this gene could have arisen as a mutation among the native ponies in either place at any time during their long history. However, folk belief should again be given a fair hearing. It may be that the

mutation for white markings first occurred on Iceland and came to the Shetland Islands as a deliberate import. Pied ponies may at that time have been particularly admired, as they still are by gypsies and many others.

Deliberate 'improvements'

In 1837 a grey Arab stallion was run on the island of Fetlar. His influence on the local ponies was said to have been visible in the high proportion of grey ponies on Fetlar. Later in the nineteenth century another Arab stallion was brought in, and later still a Highland pony stallion. At the time the Douglases were writing (1912) there were two distinct breeds of ponies on Fetlar: true Shetlands and a larger type (11-13 hands). It seems that the real Shetlands were very little affected by the newcomers.

13

Unfortunate attempts to bring in larger ponies were recorded in the *New Statistical Account of the Shetland Islands* in 1841:

> A pernicious practice has too much prevailed of crossing with larger and incongruous breeds from Scotland; and the progeny, as might have been expected, displays all the bad points, with few of the good, of the parents. A natural but rough antidote to these evils is, in some measure, to be found in bad seasons, which fall with fatal severity on the degenerate.

The clear implication is that the attempts were, and deserved to be, unsuccessful, and did not have a lasting effect on the true Shetland type.

One type or two? – or three?

No discussion of the history of the Shetland pony is complete without referring to the controversy as to whether there are two distinct types. Maurice Cox pointed out that

The two types: (*below*) The 'Scandinavian' type – Thor 83, by Odin 32, bred by the Marquis of Londonderry, foaled 1886; and (*opposite*) the 'Oriental' type – Bellman 285, by Vespa 156, bred by R. W. R. Mackenzie, foaled 1900.

in all writings prior to the mid nineteenth century there is no mention of there being more than one type; he also remarked that the earlier writers were observant and knowledgeable about livestock, and could have been expected to mention the existence of two different types if they had seen them. There is no mention of different types in Volume 1 of the Stud Book, published in 1891. Yet by the turn of the century informed opinion was that there are, and always have been, two types. R. W. R. Mackenzie, founder of the celebrated Earlshall stud in Fife, seems to be speaking from experience:

> There seems no doubt that there always were on the islands two distinct types of ponies, one a thick dray-horse type, the other more bloodlike, which may be called the saddle type. Both have intermingled freely, and one finds even after careful mating an occasional reversion from one type to another.

Dr and Mrs Douglas, whose book was the first monograph on Shetland ponies, wrote: 'The fact that the Shetland pony, as we have it today, is sometimes of a purely

Scandinavian type, sometimes of an Oriental type, may perhaps be explained by regarding it as a composite of two distinct races.' Here the Douglases are expressing in non-technical terms what a geneticist would expect to find, that the ponies are *sometimes* of one type, *sometimes* of the other. Thus the majority of ponies are somewhere in between. Further, the Douglases are doubtless right when they attribute these two types to genes brought to the population by different ancestral stocks. The majority of ponies will carry a mixture of genes from each stock and will be 'middling', but sometimes the assortment of genes in a mating will produce a pony with a concentration of one rather than the other. This is what is referred to by Mackenzie when he finds 'occasional reversion from one type to another', and by the Douglases when they say elsewhere: 'Shetland ponies of this Oriental type do not form continuous or separate strains within the breed, but crop out here and there, sometimes the parents, and sometimes the progeny, of ponies apparently purely Scandinavian.'

It has also been suggested that there have always been three distinct types: the two mentioned above, and the miniature. Although it is certainly true that there have always been very small ponies on the Islands (as is recorded in the *Statistical Account* of 1841) they were not a separate type, they occurred as one end of a continuum. Of course a pony under 34 inches high is noticeably small, and would be likely to catch the eye among a group of larger ponies, but it is also true that there are (and always have been) many ponies of 35, 36 and 37 inches, so that there is no gap between the small type and the standard Shetland pony. However, some breeders are now making the attempt to set up separate strains of ponies under 34 inches high, and it is well possible that they will eventually create a clear gap between miniatures and standard ponies. (This will be discussed further in chapter 8.)

Photographs taken in the Shetland Islands in the late nineteenth century show every conceivable variation between the three types we have been discussing. It might not be unfair to say that one of the most frequent is a pony with a heavy coarse head, upright shoulder, light bone and goose rump – not a sort that one would want to accept as one of the 'types' of the breed!

2 The Shetland pony in the nineteenth century

Shetland ponies suddenly came to the attention of the outside world in the nineteenth century, in two quite different ways.

Creatures of fashion

Firstly, Shetlands became fashionable with the English nobility. Sometimes the ponies were used as decorative park animals, making a change from the usual fallow deer, and being easier to fence in. One such herd belonged to the Marquis of Bristol, at Ickworth, Suffolk. Records of his ponies, all black, go as far back as 1815.

At the same time, Shetlands were considered extremely smart as harness ponies. The Marchioness of Salisbury was one of the most distinguished ladies of her time, and set the tone for elegant society even when she was in her eighties; she went everywhere in a phaeton drawn by four black Shetland ponies, with postillions and outriders. This was in the 1830s.

The cornerstone of the Shetland pony's prestige was royal patronage. Her Majesty Queen Victoria kept several Shetlands. At Holyrood she had a chestnut and white pair, which she had bought for £14 10s from Mr Laurenson of Lerwick, and at Windsor she had a pair of duns or creams bred by Mr Balfour of Balfour Castle on Shapinsay (in the Orkneys). Her Majesty's Shetlands drew a phaeton in which she took her exercise in Windsor Park. These ponies grew into a royal tradition. The Queen's daughter, HRH The Princess Victoria, also had a phaeton with a pair of Shetlands. She chose a pair of two different colours, which was considered in those days to make a smarter pair than the matched colours that are almost the rule today.

Shetlands were not only fashionable, they were economical too, not just in the amount of food they required but in running expenses. Among the many taxes imposed to raise funds for the Napoleonic Wars were taxes on working horses and on carriages. These were on a sliding scale, with large horses and carriages being charged most, and very small ponies and their vehicles being exempt. A gentleman might indulge his wife in a pair of Shetland ponies and a phaeton by reflecting that there would be no duty to pay.

The ideal pony for children

Shetland ponies were also the height of fashion as children's ponies. More and more

HRH The Princess Victoria in her phaeton drawn by a pair of Shetland ponies

children were learning to ride (sons and daughters of newly rich manufacturers and merchants, as well as little lords and ladies), and the Shetland was considered the ideal mount.

Sir Walter Gilbey, one of the most knowledgeable horsemen ever, was a keen supporter of Shetlands:

> The docility and good temper of the Shetland pony make him, above all, the best and most trustworthy mount for a child. Captain H. Hayes has remarked that 'a comparatively high degree of mental (*i.e.*, reasoning) power is not desirable in a horse, because it is apt to make him impatient of control by man'. The Shetland pony is the rule-proving exception; for he combines with the highest order of equine intelligence a disposition curiously free from vice or trickiness.

Sir Walter had a famous Shetland pony of his own, called Good Friday, who won a number of first prizes in the 1890s. Young children were often mounted on ponies such as these. There was a fashion for loading babies into panniers, baskets mounted on each side of a pack saddle. The infants either faced forwards or sat back-to-back, and if one was much heavier, weights were used for balance. Donkeys were considered safest for this work, but ponies were classier, and Shetlands were best of all because mother or nurse did not have to lift the babies so far.

Frank Townend Barton, another of the great nineteenth-century horsemen, was equally sure about the suitability of the breed as a first mount: 'There is no better variety of pony for a child than a Shetlander', but he did not start the riders off so young. With a surprising streak of feminism he wrote:

> By the time that a child reaches ten years or thereabout it ought to be able to control a well-mannered Shetland pony whilst in the saddle, and the sooner a child is taught to look after herself (or himself) a little, the better horseman it will become.

Sir Walter Gilbey's Shetland pony Good Friday, here being ridden by a very small boy in a basket saddle. Some children started riding even younger than this.

19

A country ride. The child with the long flowing curls is a boy; a girl would have ridden side-saddle.

'A chip of the old block' – a cartoon from *Punch*.

Children were encouraged to go hunting, even though it was (and is) one of the most dangerous of sports. Shetlands were evidently thought of as miniature hunters, as described by a leading sportsman, Digby Collins:

> The withers high and the shoulders long, in order to enable him to rise well at his fences, as well as to clear the obstacles that may come across him, in the shape of ridge and furrow, drains, hillocks, &c.; the hips and pelvis should be broad, with deep back ribs and powerful loins, in order that he may be able to dash his haunches under him at a big jump. I have seen these 'points' intensely developed in a pony 10 hands high.

The export trade

In the first half of the nineteenth century rather over a hundred ponies a year were leaving the Islands. By the middle of the century exports had increased immensely. There were several factors involved, apart from the demand noted above. One was improved transport within Britain; up till then ponies had been transported 'on the hoof' along poor roads (the ponies that went to the Marquis of Bristol's estate at Ickworth travelled by ship to Hull and then some 120 miles to their new home along roads sometimes no better than cart-tracks). With the building of railways, canals, and macadamised roads trade became much easier.

Another factor was America. Since gaining its independence from Britain at the end of the eighteenth century, the new country had become immensely prosperous. The Americans wanted to have – and could afford to pay for – everything that was best about the genteel British way of life, and high on their list was British horseflesh of all shapes and sizes. This of course included Shetland ponies. Large numbers of Shetlands crossed the Atlantic.

The coal mines

Meanwhile, another entirely different demand for Shetlands had arisen. It nearly wiped them out, but in the long run proved to be their salvation.

In the 1830s an energetic philanthropist, Lord Ashley, began to campaign for better working conditions in the coal mines. His efforts led to the passing of the Mines Act 1842, which among other things said that children under the age of ten and women could no longer be employed underground. This was predictably unpopular with the employers, who evaded the law whenever they could, but it led to a dramatic increase

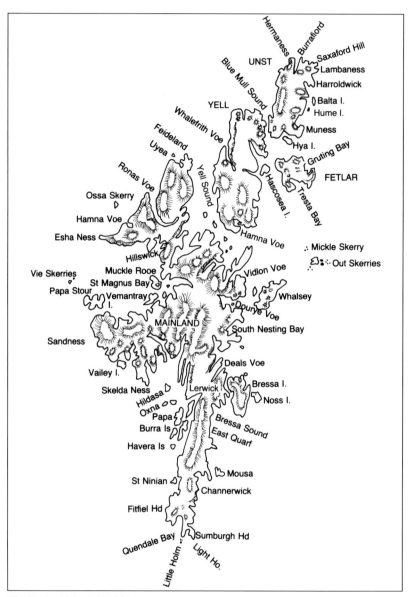

The Shetland Islands in 1856.

in demand for pit ponies. There are three stages in transporting coal out of a mine: from coal-face to haulage road, along haulage road to pit bottom, and from pit bottom to surface. Previously, ponies (not Shetlands) had been used on the haulage roads, while the coal had been brought from the coal-face by women and children dragging sledges. From 1842 things had to change, and ponies began to work at the face. Smaller ponies were better, because they could get into the narrower seams. Low and strong, Shetlands seemed purpose-built for the job, and they were first tried out in a few mines in County Durham in the mid 1840s. Their use spread very rapidly, particularly as mine-owners discovered that they were actually more economical than human labour: they did more work per day, had a longer working lifetime, and cost less to feed even than the meagre wages of women and children. The pit-ponies' work is described in chapter 4.

Demand exceeds supply

The sudden demand for ponies for the mines had a catastrophic effect on the Shetland Islands. For one thing, it occurred at a time when there was terrible poverty among the islanders after the potato famine. Then the price of wool went up, as the mechanised mills in northern England got into their stride, which tempted a number of land-owners to evict crofters in order to establish sheep-walks. Various schemes were devised to provide employment, including the building of the first roads in the Islands. But the crofters remained on the edge of subsistence, and their ponies were the only thing they had to sell. Up till the Mines Act of 1842, demand for the ponies was patchy. The ponies going to the aristocrats in England and Scotland were often sent by Shetland gentry, not crofters. The latter would be lucky if they could sell a pony to a Dutch fisherman.

The unfortunate effect of the unsteady demand was that the crofters would sell which ponies they could, that is, the best ones. That left them with the poorer stock to breed from, so that the next generation was poorer still. Matters were made worse by the fact that breeding herds were left to their own devices. All the ponies were turned out on to the scattald (common grazings) for the summer, and the mares were served by whatever stallion happened to be around, or were not served at all if there were none. Foals were not weaned in the autumn but left on their dam through their first winter. This caused the mares to abort their next year's foals, so that they were raising a foal only every other year.

Such was the situation when the Islands were hit by the sudden urgent demand for ponies for the mines. There were perhaps 10,000 ponies on the Islands: suddenly, hundreds of ponies were wanted each year. In 1858 some 400 were bought by a single dealer, and in 1861 more than 700 left the Islands. Only male ponies went to the mines (mares would have been equally capable of doing the work but it was thought that keeping mares stabled underground with the entires would lead to trouble). Dealers moved in, not just to buy colts and stallions from the crofters but to fix up various arrangements giving them a stake in the booming market. Sometimes the system was 'halvers', under which the dealer provided a brood mare in return for a half-share in her offspring. More often dealers would advance a crofter cash or goods against an expected foal.

Prices leapt up. At the start of the trade, ponies cost £4 10s each including delivery to the colliery; by 1861 they were £10 or £12 in the Islands. The quality of the ponies went down. So did their numbers. By 1871 the pony population had been reduced to 2,247 'unbroken horses and mares, kept solely for breeding'. If some 1,500 of these were mares, having a foal every other year, that would be 750 foals a year, of which half would be colts, that is, 375. The mine-owners wanted something like a thousand ponies a year. This was a crisis, and the first person to recognise it was the Marquis of Londonderry.

Lord Londonderry

The Marquis was a mine-owner, whose collieries in County Durham had been among the earliest to use Shetland ponies. He was pleased with the work the ponies did, and had no intention of letting the supply dry up, or of settling for the inferior ponies that were coming onto the market. In 1870 he leased the islands of Bressay and Noss, and he employed Mr J. J. R. Meiklejohn to manage the stud there. Mr Robert Brydon was to manage the ponies at Lord Londonderry's stud at Seaham Harbour, County Durham. Their brief was to breed ponies with 'as much weight as possible and as near the ground as it can be got'. They had to start by combing through the depleted and weedy herds of the crofters, picking out any ponies, mares or stallions, that seemed to them to be of the right type or in that direction. They did not mind what colour the ponies were if the conformation was right (the Shetland fraternity came to believe that Meiklejohn and Brydon had selected blacks only, as the Londonderry type later turned out to be predominantly black, but this was not so). No expense was spared in buying the foundation stock or in laying out the grounds on the islands. Mares were kept in enclosures on Bressay, while the stallions and colts had their bachelor quarters on Noss (much the smaller island). Foals were weaned in the autumn, and ran with the rest of the youngstock on the hills for the winter, being

Jack 16, breeder unknown, believed foaled in 1871. This stallion founded the most important blood line in the Londonderry Stud, and therefore in the breed as a whole.

given hay but not shelter. The mares, also fed on hay in the winter, were grouped into bunches of twelve or fifteen to run with a stallion for the summer.

The enterprise was a great success. Through careful selection of the right stocks and a well-planned scheme of inbreeding (breeding a lot more closely than most people would care to nowadays, but scientifically perfectly right), a well-defined type of pony soon emerged, and became known as the Londonderry type. It was just what the Marquis had wanted: heavily made, broad in chest, back and quarters, short in the leg with excellent bone and good round feet. Some had prophesied that with the winter feeding at Bressay the ponies would grow taller than the original stock, but in fact over the years the average height of the Londonderry ponies went down, as smaller ponies were being selectively bred.

As an enlightened policy, Lord Londonderry allowed the crofters on Bressay to run their mares with some of his stallions, so that the improvements in the breed were spread a little more widely. Dealers realised that better colts would fetch better prices, and began to invest in improving the crofters' stock. Having bought up all the available colt foals, they would choose for a future stallion the best pit type among them and leave him on the Islands to run with the crofters' mares.

Other land-owners followed Lord Londonderry's example and set up studs in which both stallions and mares were chosen for quality and proper records were kept. Mr John Bruce had ponies in three places – on Mousa Island, at Sumburgh, and on Fair Isle – and he used stallions from one stud on mares at another, to keep the best blood evenly distributed. Several breeders on Unst, traditionally the island with the best ponies, also began to breed systematically. They included Mr Alexander Sandison of Uyeasound and the Marquis of Zetland. Mr Anderson Manson's herd at Laxfirth, just north of Lerwick, was one of the largest in the Islands, and of excellent quality. Messrs John Anderson and Sons owned a lot of land around Hillswick, at the northern end of the Mainland, and their stallions were also available for the crofters' mares.

The foundation of the Stud Book

These gentlemen fully realised the value of the type of pony they had worked ten or twenty years to establish, and they saw that to form a Shetland Pony Stud-Book Society and to keep a register of all ponies in a Stud Book was the only way to protect this asset. The Society was formed in 1890; the first President, appropriately, was the Marquis of Londonderry. There were 111 members, mostly crofters. The first volume of the Stud Book was published in 1891, from the Society's offices in Aberdeen. (Although the Society has always felt the Islands to be its spiritual home, its actual home has been at one place or another in Scotland.) It was the first stud book for a native breed to be published in Britain, but it was able to model itself on the stud books of other breeds, such as the Shire, that had recently been started up. In it were entered 408 mares who had had a foal prior to 1 September 1890, and 48 stallions foaled before 1 January 1886. The criteria for a pony's eligibility were that it was under 42 inches at four years old and that it had been born in the Shetland Islands, or if it had not, that it was of reputed Shetland origin and had been sired by a pony bred in the Islands.

Difficulties of organisation meant that only a small proportion of the Shetland ponies eligible for it were entered in the first volume of the Stud Book. Oddly, there were hardly any from the island of Unst, even though there were numerous keen breeders there. Most of the ponies did not have a recorded pedigree going back for more than a single generation (if that, for there were many cases in which the sire was unknown) but some that came from studs where systematic records had been kept, notably Lord Londonderry's, had two or more generations of pedigree behind them when the Stud Book began.

The first volume of the Stud Book also contained several interesting articles by experts. James Goudie wrote on 'The Early History of the Shetland Pony', J. J. R. Meiklejohn on 'Its Breeding and Management', and Robert Brydon on 'Employment after Leaving Shetland'. Brydon summarised the importance of the pit-pony trade, comparing the present situation with that of 1851, when thirty male ponies three to five years old were sold to collieries in Durham at £4 10s each delivered:

> Since then the ponies have increased to an enormous extent. Average yearlings are now worth, in the north of England, £15 per head; two-year-olds, £18; and older ponies are scarcely obtainable. The price is governed in a great degree by the size. The smaller they are – *coeteris paribus* – the more money they are worth. A good four-year-old, 9.2, will fetch, on an average, £10 more than one five or six inches higher. This is, no doubt, partly owing to fancy, but chiefly to the small ponies being available for work in thin coal seams where larger ones cannot enter. The sheltie being the smallest breed of ponies (and, so far as I am aware, the only breed which boasts of ponies under ten hands), it follows that they have the market all to themselves.
>
> The wisdom of limiting the height of ponies admissible to the Stud-Book to 10.2 and under cannot be too highly commended, as it will tend to make breeders more careful in the selection and mating of their mares. When Shetland ponies are above 10.2, they come into competition with Welsh and foreign ponies, and the price suffers accordingly.

It could not have been more clearly put: the purpose of the Stud Book was to keep the size of the ponies down, because only in that way could their dominance of the market be maintained. Thus it was that the demands of the coalmining trade ensured the survival of the Shetland pony as it originally was in prehistoric times and as it still is today.

3 The great breeders

The Londonderry type of Shetland was *the* type for the breed. Londonderry ponies were overwhelmingly successful in the show ring: at the twelve shows of the Highland and Agricultural Society held between 1900 and 1911 there were 116 first and second prizes awarded, of which 114 went to ponies sired by stallions from the Londonderry stud.

It is worth looking at how the Londonderry plan of inbreeding worked. The key figure was the stallion Jack 16. He was black, and 40 inches high (tall for a Londonderry pony); he lived to be thirty years old, working at stud all his life. He had three outstanding sons, and the four of them together made up the main bloodline. The sons, all black, were (1) Odin 32, of the same type as Jack but smaller at 38 inches; (2) Laird of Noss 20, also 38 inches but more lightly built; and (3) Lord of the Isles 26, the smallest at 36 inches but the most heavily built of the brothers. Jack and his three sons sired 248 out of the first 490 foals registered as produce of the stud, and a further 160 were by Jack's grandsons. The daughters of Jack and of his sons were almost always mated to either their own sire or to one of their brothers (full or half).

But there was another male blood line, that of Prince of Thule 36. A brown 36 inches high, he was of a type quite different from Jack. He can be thought of as the only representative in the Londonderry stud of the 'Oriental' type, as opposed to

Prince of Thule 36, breeder unknown, believed foaled in 1872.

Jack's line which was of 'Scandinavian' type. Prince of Thule was used on daughters of Jack, and also daughters of Odin, perhaps to put back some of the quality that might otherwise have been sacrificed in the search for weight-near-the-ground. The system, then, was to inbreed as closely as possible to the Jack line, with occasional outcrosses to the Prince of Thule line, the resulting mares being put back to the Jack line again. It was also policy to put the mares to a different horse nearly every year. As an example, the foundation mare Darling 174 (by Jack) had her first three foals by the three different brothers.

It was brilliantly successful breeding. The Douglases do not overstate when they say that the results were a degree of breed improvement without a parallel in the equine world. By the late 1890s the future seemed rosy: the breed had been saved from near extinction, the Stud Book was established, sales were still high. The Shetland pony world was shattered in 1899 by the news that Lord Londonderry had lost his lease of Bressay and Noss, and that the whole stud was to be sold up.

The Londonderry dispersal sale

One hundred and fifty ponies were sold at the Londonderry dispersal sale on 7 September 1899. The sale was held at Seaham Harbour rather than on Shetland, because most of the buyers were expected to be from the mainland (only a dozen ponies went back to the Islands). The average price was just over 20 guineas (£21), the equivalent in 1995 terms of £1,250, and the top price was 125 guineas (now over £8,000). Among the purchasers were the Lady Estella and Lady Dorothea Hope, daughters of the 6th Earl of Hopetoun, of Hopetoun House, Linlithgow. They were founder members of the Stud-Book Society, even though they had already moved to the south of England. They had previously acquired the elegant Prince of Thule (by this time dead) and his son Oman, and at the dispersal sale they paid 52 guineas for Jack's son Odin, aged nineteen years. They bought twelve ponies in all, and this was almost the last time they brought ponies into their stud, all later breeding being done from home-bred stock.

The Ladies' substantial purchases were outnumbered by those of Mr Robert Mackenzie, another founder member of the Society. He owned the Earlshall stud in Fife, and at the Londonerry sale he bought fifteen ponies, all female. His stud was one of the largest, and he was registering over thirty foals a year. His ponies were taller on average than the Londonderry stock and he was particularly interested in breeding colours. He brought in a grey stallion from the Islands, and later he himself bred the most important of all the chestnut sires, Emillius of Earlshall 1121.

Odin 32 (*above*), by Jack 16, bred by the Marquis of Londonderry, foaled 1880. (*Opposite page, top*) Marquis of Earlshall, bred by R. W. R. Mackenzie; and (*bottom*) Bard of Transy, bred by D. W. H. Dick and owned by Mrs V. Hampton. This distinguished stud traces back to ponies bought at the Londonderry dispersal sale.

Mr William Mungall bought the entire foundation stock for his Transy stud at the Londonderry dispersal sale. He bought a stallion, Hector 183, and five female ponies. From the outset he was interested in a quality type of pony that would be suitable for riding and driving, rather than the purpose-built pit-pony that the Londonderry type basically was. The present-day Transy stud, owned by Mr Dougal Dick, is a direct continuation of this stud, and the emphasis on performance has remained.

Other important breeders of that time included Dr Douglas, who started his stud in 1902 using mainly Londonderry-bred stock but aiming for a lighter type of pony. Mrs Hobart of Southampton purchased several stallions from Lady Estella Hope, and ponies from her stud were successfully shown in hand and in harness; a number was exported to Australia. Mrs Houldsworth of Kirkbride, Ayrshire, began to breed

Shetlands in 1909. She concentrated on the classic Londonderry type, which was still being bred in the stud up until the death of her son Sir Reginald Houldsworth in 1989. Just before the 1914–18 war, Mr Kerr of Harviestoun added Shetlands to his list of interests: he was already a noted breeder of Clydesdales, Hackneys, and Aberdeen Angus cattle. He based his stud on Transy and Earlshall stock, and his breeding has had a considerable influence on later show ponies.

The other stud book

During the boom years of the Shetland pony trade, the Council of the Stud-Book Society decided to close the Stud Book; that is, from that time it would be impossible to register any pony whose parents were not already in the Book. That happened in 1905. But before long the crofter-breeders were in difficulties; they had not bothered to register their mares with the Society, and now they found, to their chagrin, that they were unable to export stock to Canada and America, both of which required incoming ponies to have registration papers.

In 1908 a rival organisation was set up – the Shetland Islands Stud Book Society. Conditions for entering a pony in its Stud Book were much less stringent than for the original Stud Book. Any pony belonging to a person living in the Islands was eligible, and the pony could be taller (43 inches at four years old or 41 inches at three, which might well make bigger than 43). This was good enough for the Canadian Board of Agriculture, who accepted many ponies imported with these papers. Luckily America did not follow suit. The real Stud-Book Society came to its senses, and reopened their Stud Book in 1910, inspecting and registering 427 new mares in a single year. The rival Society withered away.

The bad years

During the First World War, demand for Shetland ponies fell dramatically. A few male ponies were still wanted for the mines, but females were virtually unsaleable. No one was buying ponies for pleasure, and the export market disappeared altogether and scarcely picked up even when the war was over. The most notable casualty of this slump was the Hillswick stud run by the Andersons, founder members of the Society. Before the war they had been selling 130 ponies a year off the Islands, but in 1919 they went bust. They were followed in the early 1920s by Mr Sandison of Unst, another leading light of the Society, and in 1927 Mr Bruce disposed of his ponies from Mousa, Sumburgh and Fair Isle.

Shetland ponies were no longer fashionable. Although horse-drawn transport was still important everywhere, the car had made its entrance and was vastly more interesting than any pony to people who wanted to cut a dash. Shetlands fell out of favour as riding ponies too. Welsh ponies had risen in popularity, and the fashion for children's ponies was for that leggier type. Many books on riding written in the 1920s and 1930s have a derisive comment to make about Shetlands: 'I omit from riding ponies the Shetland, for he is too small for practical purposes', wrote no less an authority than R. S. Summerhayes.

Yet the quality of Shetland ponies was not only as good as it had been in the boom years at the beginning of the century, it had become even better as the 'riding type' favoured by Dr Douglas, Mr Mungall and Mr Mackenzie became more prevalent. But the prices these ponies fetched were heartbreaking. Breeding stock could be had for £3 or £4 a head in England, but mares and fillies in the Islands were completely unsaleable, as their value was less than the cost of shipping them to Aberdeen.

When Mr Mackenzie retired he dispersed his prestigious Earlshall stud. It is salutory to compare the prices that were fetched that day, 23 November 1932, with those at the Londonderry dispersal. Ninety-six ponies were sold for a total of £643 18s 3d, an average of only £6 14s 1d (1997 equivalent about £200). And those were absolutely top-class ponies, the finest in the breed.

Breeders undaunted

It is astonishing that Shetland breeders should persevere in such discouraging conditions; but they did. Lady Estella Hope, whose sister Dorothea had died in 1927, moved from Kent to Sussex to South Park which gave its name to her stud (though she never used it as a prefix to ponies' names). South Park is now usually associated with miniature ponies and indeed these ponies are of a most striking type which has been of great influence and benefit at the small end of the breed. But the Ladies Hope were always equally interested in larger ponies, and bred very good ponies around 37 or 38 inches, black as well as coloured. Attractive colour has always been a South Park hallmark, going right back to the legendary foundation mare, Hoplemuroma, who was roan (see chapter 6 for her exploits in harness). Very many of the roan ponies in the show ring today have South Park ancestry; virtually all of the roan miniatures do. Another characteristic South Park colouring is white socks, which give a most attractive extra touch to a harness pony.

Mr Mungall of Transy continued to breed and show; his confidence in the breed was unshakeable. When he died in 1936 his daughter, Mrs William Dick, took over and carried on with the same confidence. Mr Kerr of Harviestoun also went on with his breeding and showing, taking his ponies to the major shows along with his cattle. But Mrs Duffus, who had begun her stud in about 1910 and had achieved great success in the show ring, particularly with her black stallion Dibblitz of Penniwells, sold all her ponies in 1932.

Several important new studs were started in the 1920s and 1930s. Probably the most influential was that of Betty Cox, wife of Major Maurice Cox. Her stud was founded at Marshwood in Dorset, and only moved to Kirkcudbrightshire after the Second World War. She aimed for, and achieved, a type of pony remarkable for its free action and prolific mane and tail.

Another highly important stud was founded by Miss A. Ritchie at Broadshade, Aberdeenshire; her Netherley ponies were like the original Londonderry type, black and with great substance. Mrs Atkinson's Felbridge stud in Surrey specialised in coloured ponies. Based on Earlshall blood lines, her breeding achieved the quality usually associated with black ponies but in chestnut and grey.

A Marshwood line: Jilt of Marshwood, bred by Mrs M. C. Cox, with three of her daughters – Knock Jubilee Day, Knock Jessamine, and Knock Juliette, bred by Mrs D. Edwards.

The Second World War dealt another blow to these studs. Wartime regulations were imposed that required land to be used for food production wherever possible. Shetlands had not sunk so low as to be regarded as food, so they had to make way for sheep. Some studs lost their grazing altogether; sometimes breeders were able to board out ponies here and there until better times came and breeding could start again. This happened with the Transy stud, which was not able to set up again until 1954. Major Cox recalled that of the fifty ponies at Marshwood at the beginning of the war only seven were left at the end.

Once again the breed survived. Indeed the post-war economic recovery all round the world benefited Shetland ponies as much as anyone else. Suddenly people wanted riding ponies for their children again, and Shetland ponies were back in favour for this. One of their keenest supporters (though not herself a breeder) was Miss Glenda Spooner, founder of Ponies of Britain: 'They are excellent and reliable, while in harness their speed and endurance is astonishing.' The Americans and Canadians once more came over to buy Shetland ponies, in dozens rather than hundreds, but as before they wanted quality and would pay for it.

Post-war studs

A number of new breeders established studs in this more cheerful climate for Shetlands. Mr H. P. Sleigh, whose father had had a stud before the First World War, began his Wells stud at Fyvie, Aberdeenshire, in 1948. The importance of this stud cannot be overstated. Breeding closely and aiming for the short-coupled Londonderry pony, Mr Sleigh had the most phenomenal success in the show ring. Wells ponies have won the championship at the Royal Highland Show twenty-five times and the Royal (English) sixteen times. Often enough when Mr Sleigh has not shown the champion the title has gone to a pony bred from Wells stock. The Wells type is much the heaviest-built among Shetland ponies, with phenomenal bone; there has been some criticism that they are *too* heavily built to be really good movers, but this is a quibble in view of the unquestionable correctness of these ponies. They are not as large as they look: for example the great Wells Manifesto, winner of both the Royal titles, was only 38$^1/_2$ inches high.

Other highly important studs dating from the 1940s were those of Mr T. H. F. Myles of Fife (Highfield), whose ponies were also black but were taller and lighter than the Wells type, with Marshwood as well as Wells ancestry, Mr I. Dishington of Kendal (Lakeland), who bred bays, chestnuts and roans most of which traced back to Inspected Stock mares that Mr Dishington had bought off the Islands, Miss E. Smith

The late T. H. F. Myles, founder of the Highfield Stud, seen here with his mare Highfield Bramble, aged thirty.

of Scalloway (Berry), who originally bred middle-sized black ponies though she now breeds coloured miniatures, and Mrs S. C. Swannack (Woodbury), a driving enthusiast whose black and bay ponies had South Park forebears.

More studs were established in the 1950s. Among the names whose ponies figure in the breeding of the best ponies today are: Mrs K. Amers of Moretonhampstead (Luckdon), black ponies based on a judicious mixture of Harviestoun/Netherley stock with Marshwood blood for the quality of action; Miss A. Edge of Kendal (Hutton), whose grey ponies are the ancestors of the best greys seen today; Mr W. Shillibeer of Yelverton (Lakehead), winner of a number of titles at both the Royals with ponies bred from Wells, Harviestoun and Transy lines; Mrs Greaves of Dumfries (Ebony), middle-sized black ponies of a distinctive type with no Wells background but some Kirkbride and Harviestoun blood; the Misses Salter and French of Guildford (Hurtwood), ponies bred for driving with Marshwood and Felbridge ancestry; Mrs M. J. King of Painswick (Donnachaidh); Mrs H. Hyde of Callander (Braes of Greenock), and Mr and Mrs R. Gosling of Stowmarket (Wetherden); the last three all breeding classic black ponies with varying amounts of Wells input.

With the increased interest in showing in the 1960s (see chapter 7) new breeders based their top-quality studs upon these earlier lines. These keen exhibitors included the Duchess of Devonshire (Chatsworth), Mrs G. Knight of Wantage (Lockinge), Mrs E. House of Bridgwater (Bincombe) and Mr and Mrs J. Church of Hadlow

36

Down (Nashes), all of whom achieved the distinction of winning the championship at the Royal Show. The Chatsworth ponies were black, based on Wells, Harviestoun and Transy lines; many were by the notable sire Braes of Greenock Valiant (the Duchess also bred miniature ponies with South Park ancestry). The equally distinguished Lockinge ponies were chestnut and bay as well as black; their breeding was without Wells blood, Mrs Knight preferring the Marshwood type. Other important breeders beginning at that time were Mrs D. W. J. O'Brien of Nutley (Annwood), Mrs A. W. R. Houghton of Melton Mowbray (Sysonby), and Mrs P. Lory of Basingstoke (Southley), who bred of greys and chestnuts, many sired by Tempest of Hutton.

At about that time miniature Shetlands began to be a force to be reckoned with, and the doyens among their breeders were Lionel Hamilton-Renwick of Newmarket (Birling) and Mrs C. Berry of Melrose (Firth). Chestnut colouring, especially with flaxen mane and tail, was a feature in both these studs.

Notable breeders starting in the 1970s included Mesdames J. A. and J. R.

Chatsworth Darkie, bred and owned by the Duchess of Devonshire.

37

Lockinge Edward, bred by Mrs Guy Knight and owned by Mrs V. Hampton.

Southley Bluebird, bred by Mrs P. Lory and owned by Mrs S. Helps.

Bincombe Poppy, bred and owned by Mrs E. House.

Stevenson of Hose and Mrs D. V. M. Howell of Ropley (Dewland); both these studs bred classic black ponies, with Wells foundation stock. Mrs M. Martin, of Peterhead, can scarcely be said to have started at that time, as she was raised among Shetland ponies in the Sleigh family, but her own Westpark stud (founded of course upon Wells breeding) began to come into its own. Ponies from all these three studs have won championships at the Royal and/or Royal Highland shows. Mrs D. Edwards of Appleby (Knock) has been influential in breeding quality coloured stock (Marshwood/Lakeland foundation), including probably the finest broken-coloured ponies ever seen in the breed.

In spite of the enormous expansion in showing during the 1980s, no new pre-eminent studs emerged. But there was more interest in the breeding of performance ponies. One of the first breeders to turn attention to this was Mrs D. Staveley, of Driffield (Eastlands), whose ponies were star attractions in show driving in the 1980s. At the same time, Annwood ponies (bred by Mrs O'Brien) have always been successful in performance, particularly under saddle, and continue to be so. Another name of note in performance ponies is Mrs C. Logan's Riccalton stud.

As the pattern of the Shetland world in the 1990s takes shape, it is still the case that no new breeders can claim the success of the classic studs named above. The top prizes in the show ring continue to go to ponies bred by people who began in the

Mrs C. Berry's colt foal by Firth Gold-n-Ivory.

Hose Element, bred and owned by Mesdames J. A. and J. R. Stevenson. She was the Champion at the Royal Show and Supreme Champion at the Annual Breed Show in 1992 as a two-year-old, and was again Supreme Champion at the Annual Breed Show the following year (shown here).

Annwood ponies head the line: Glimpse of Annwood and Gilia of Annwood, bred by Mrs D. W. J. O'Brien, standing first and second in the Leading Rein class at the Autumn Shetland Pony Show 1992.

1970s or earlier, even though they are breeding far fewer ponies now than they did then. The situation will inevitably change when these senior breeders retire, but it is not yet clear what the Shetland 'names' of the turn of the century will be.

4 Shetland ponies at work

Shetland ponies are made for work: they are, relative to their size, by far the strongest equines in the world. In their native islands, their work was originally twofold, to do all the hard labour on the crofts and to be the only means of transport.

All-purpose transport

Up until the 1840s there were no roads of any kind in the Shetland Islands. Apart from boats, ponies were the only means of carrying things and people from one place to another. The earliest account of their use is from a clergyman living in the Islands in the seventeenth century: he reported that 'The Horses are of a little size and excellent Mettell: for one of them will easily carry a man or woman 20 miles a day.' As well as crofters, the gentry used to ride the local ponies, and Sir Walter Scott, a great enthusiast for everything Shetland, has given a wonderful description of a mount for a lady:

> One of them . . . was decorated with a huge side-saddle of venerable antiquity – a mass, as it were, of cushion and padding, from which depended, on all sides, a housing of ancient tapestry, which, having been originally intended for a horse of ordinary size, covered up the diminutive palfrey over whom it was spread, from the ears to the tail, and from the shoulder to the fetlock, leaving nothing visible but its head, which looked fiercely out from these enfoldments, like the heraldic representation of a lion looking out of a bush.

Once roads were built on Shetland, ponies were also used in harness. Whether or not this was an improvement can be guessed from a comment written some fifty years on, by an ornithologist visiting the Islands in 1895: 'At Voe the mails are changed over and I found that the $6^1/_2$ miles between Voe and Brae must be walked as the mail-gig was a dilapidated old box affair with a small pony and string-fastened harness.'

Work on the crofts

The work that ponies did on the crofts is very much a living tradition on the Islands, even though machines have now entirely taken over. Many people can give first-hand accounts of what it was like to work on the family croft with ponies as the only form of power.

By far the most important task was 'flitting' the peats. The peat was cut by hand, in late May or June; a special spade called a tushkar was used, and the peat was cut into neat slabs and laid out in rows. That was men's work. Women's work was to turn the slabs to cure them, which took two or three weeks, with the rows being turned every few days. Then came the ponies, led by boys, to carry or flit the peat to the croft; this might be several miles away as the peat banks tended to be up in the hills (it is quite different from the bog peat of Ireland).

The gear for the ponies consisted of a pad (flackie) of woven straw usually with

Ponies flitting the peats on Fetlar, in the 1920s. (Photo reproduced by kind permission of the Shetland Museum.)

a sack or some wool under it. On that went a wooden pack-saddle called a klibber, with hinged sides held together by two wooden bars (nugs) which crossed at the top and projected so that the load could be hooked on to them. The klibber was held on by a bellyband (wime-girt) attached to a loop of rope at the bottom of each of the panels, and there was also a crupper (tail-girt).

The load of peat was put into a pair of baskets (keshies) made of plaited straw or rushes and one handle of the keshie was hooked on to the nug. To stop lumps of peat falling out, a net (maishie) was used; it went on top of the klibber, underneath the keshie, and was hooked up over the nug on the other side. The same gear was used for the various other loads that the ponies carried on the crofts, which included potatoes, hay and seaweed (used as a fertiliser on the fields). Pack ponies were also used in the fish-curing industry, carrying barrels of salt outwards and barrels of cured fish back to Lerwick for export.

Mr Bobby Laurenson of Bridge of Walls recounted that the ponies that worked on the crofts were quite big, at least 40 inches high, and that two ponies of that size were strong enough to pull a plough. Progress was slow, but the area on a croft that had to be ploughed was only an acre or two.

Two klibbers. The one with two pairs of nugs is the more usual type. (These are from the collections of the Walls Museum.)

The late Mrs E. Hall's mare Merrylegs pictured at work on the croft at Walls in 1968; she is drawing a load of hay in a net.

The same pony performing the same task fifteen years later; this time the load will go by cart. (The hay can be seen in the foreground of the picture.)

But an account in the *Shetland Advertiser* of 1862 states that it was usual to plough with a team of four ponies:

> They generally begin their labours at 6 o'clock in the morning and continue for two, three or four hours only, as the horses are soon exhausted. If they have another change of ponies they take them out to the field at 10 o'clock and plough to 12 o'clock. After dinner and at 1 o'clock they return to their labours out of doors and sow seed and harrow it, and remain thus occupied until 7 or 8 o'clock at night.

Harrowing was much lighter work. The harrow, which had wooden tines, could even be drawn by humans if need be (and many present-day Shetlanders can remember doing so as children). Harness for draught-work consisted of collar and hames, with a band or pad on the back to support the chains by which the implement was pulled.

Sometimes a cart was used for moving loads around the farm or over greater distances, if the roads or tracks were not too rough. Once again Shetlands demonstrated their enormous power.

The coal mines

The story of how Shetland ponies came to be employed in the coal mines in the nineteenth century was told in chapter 2. The pit-ponies led a hard life, but it is fair to say that they were well looked after (simply a matter of economics: a fit pony can work, an unfit one cannot). Robert Brydon, who was employed by Lord Londonderry to breed ponies for the pits, described their work:

> It is not overstating the case to say that, on an average, they will travel over 3,000 miles in the course of a year, and 'shift' as many tons of coal. This is no mean performance when we consider that the work is done in the black darkness of a coal mine, by a pony 38 inches high, working in a place very little higher than itself. The amount of work varies in different collieries; in level pits much more can be accomplished than where the gradients are steep. The lot of the pit-pony is certainly a hard one, but it is not, by any means, the dreadful existence that many suppose. Their work is hard, but they are well fed, and the equable temperature of the coal mine keeps them singularly free from all catarrhal infections, so common in animals which have to stand the vicissitudes of our British climate. As a rule, their coats are sleek, and their condition such as anyone with

A Shetland pit-pony with his 'horse-keeper'. (Photo by courtesy of British Coal.)

a stud of hunters would envy. There is a popular belief that ponies down coal mines soon go blind. This is not so; but loss of sight is not infrequent as the result of accidental injury, to which ponies, working in the dark passages, are very liable. That they occasionally are badly used goes without saying, but generally the Shetland pony, from its tractable disposition, is a favourite with its driver, the putter boy, from whom, as a rule, it receives, if rough, at least not unkindly

(*Opposite page*)
A pit-pony at work, hauling pit props in a colliery in Co. Durham in the 1970s. (Photo by courtesy of British Coal.)

treatment . . . Ponies have been known to follow their drivers like dogs, and to be as dejected as a forsaken maiden when, from any cause, they are separated from each other. Boys – and big boys, too – have wept for the loss of their ponies, killed in an accident, as though the little Shetland were a human friend.

Only the Shetland pony's wonderful patience enabled such a life to be borne. Robert Brydon could not 'recall a single instance where a Shetland pony had to be withdrawn from the pits as being wicked or unmanageable, a very frequent occurrence with other breeds'. And what courage it must have taken to keep on working in such dangerous conditions. Human workers suffered the most appalling casualty rates: 'Between 1861 and 1919 a miner was killed every six hours, seriously injured every two hours and injured badly every two or three minutes' – and there is no reason to think that it was any safer for the ponies.

Domestic service

Luckier by far were the Shetland ponies whose exile from the Islands took them to the country houses of the English gentry. They were fashionable riding and driving ponies, to be sure, but in those days before mechanisation or electricity there was much everyday work to be done:

> Then much may be claimed for them as general utility ponies, either to those who can afford nothing else, or even at a large country house. With a minimum of care and attention they are always ready for any odd job and are never sick or sorry. As anyone can drive him, the sheltie is always turned out whenever there is an errand to be run or a parcel to fetch from the station, and when not otherwise employed he can be harnessed to the mowing-machine. At one country house we know, one of his many jobs was to pump water by means of a treadmill in which he was placed for half an hour every morning. This system filled the cisterns with fresh water every day, and was found infinitely superior to the wind-mill it superseded. (Mackenzie, 1911)

Such a varied workload was probably not at all unwelcome to the ponies. No ponies lead that kind of life nowadays, but many do odd jobs around farms and

49

smallholdings. Shetland-owning mothers may be lucky enough to be able to use the pony and trap for conveying the children to and from school, as the author did.

Show business

Such an attractive creature as the Shetland pony has a natural place in the world of entertainment. Circuses have always employed Shetlands, because they are clever at learning tricks and are reliable in temperament (they never bite the audience); and the broken-colours are particularly favoured by showmen. There is a delightful story about a circus Shetland of one hundred years ago. Mr Robert Sinclair, one of the leading lights of the Lerwick Temperance Society, travelled widely on the Society's business:

> On one occasion Sinclair was in Edinburgh and went to a circus, the principal attraction of which was a Shetland pony, possessed, it was claimed, of more than ordinary equine intelligence, and which could answer questions in a most satisfactory manner. After performing one or two simple tricks, the pony was asked

Show business: Mrs S. Helps and her Shetland pair putting on the style for a wedding.

to point out the man who was very fond of a dram. Walking across to where our friend was sitting, the pony stopped before this bright and shining light of temperance, and gravely bowed its head, which Sinclair afterwards complained to a friend, was particularly hard lines coming as it did from a fellow countryman.

But circuses with animals are not now as acceptable as they once were. Show business Shetlands are more likely to be seen on the stage. There is a ready-made role for Shetland ponies in the pantomime of *Cinderella*, ideally a team of four greys to draw Cinderella in her coach to the ball. Perhaps less well known is the ballet *La Fille mal gardée*, a country love-story with a scene in which the heroine arrives in a pony cart: another natural role for a Shetland. For many years Miss Diana Grasby of the Ash Hill stud specialised in supplying ponies for these and other roles. Her mare Ashorne Seagull, a 34-inch grey, was a most accomplished performer who regularly appeared with the Royal Ballet; she passed on the family stage tradition to her daughter Ashorne Lisa.

Riding and Driving for the Disabled

No one would disagree that the most important work done today by Shetland ponies is their service with the Riding for the Disabled Association (RDA). The Association, a registered charity, was started in 1969, founded by a group of riders and medical people who had the vision that riding could provide a breakthrough in independence and self-esteem for handicapped people. The Association has been enormously successful: in 1970 there were 2,400 riders, and twenty-five years later there are over ten times that number. There are over 700 local groups holding regular sessions. Over the years there has been a great increase in the proportion of mentally rather than physically handicapped riders, and they are now in the majority at 65 per cent.

Shetland ponies are particularly well suited to the work of RDA. Their small size is a great advantage: a helper can walk beside the pony with an arm comfortably around the rider, or a person in a wheelchair can reach all over the pony, to touch it and learn its points, to groom it and pick out its feet. In some groups Shetlands specialise in being the guinea-pigs for grooming and tacking-up; bigger ponies do the actual riding lessons for adults, and Shetlands are used only for younger riders.

Driving for the Disabled began as an offshoot of RDA in 1975. Once again, the scheme was a great success. Many people, adults and children, whose disability prevented them from riding a horse or pony could get the same benefits from driving it. The seriously handicapped drivers found an exhilarating sense of freedom in being

Robin's Brae Irvine pops round the cones with disabled driver Will and able-bodied whip Wendy Knott. Robin is owned by Mrs A. Swinscow and was bred in the Islands by Mrs L. Burgess.

able to go with their pony and vehicle exactly where any able-bodied driver would go. Driving has become a significant part of the RDA's activities throughout the country, and once again Shetland ponies have come to the fore. An ordinary Shetland-sized exercise cart is often easy enough to get into for a disabled driver to be able to use it with only minor modifications, such as extra arm-rails, or else a pur-pose-built vehicle can be built for less cost than for a larger pony. A Shetland pony is so low that the disabled driver can reach to help with harnessing up or even with putting-to, slipping a lightweight shaft into the tug.

RDA horses and ponies get their chance of fame in the RDA National Championship, which began in 1979. Any animal that really knows its job is in with a chance, and small size is no problem. The ponies have to prove their manageability and good sense in every possible situation. For safety reasons, disabled riders do not take part in the competition, but are replaced with dummy riders or with light-weight adults for the ridden part of the test. The most popular part of the competition from the spectators' point of view is the 'noise and hazard test' in which the pony has to face all sorts of likely and unlikely hazards, such as suddenly opening umbrellas or falling boxes, or having to walk under a washing-line or over a sheet of polythene. Shetlands excel at this. The breed was duly proud when in the second year of the RDA Championship a Shetland pony came in Reserve Champion: he was Blue Chintz of Annwood, owned by Mrs J. Carter and bred by Mrs D. W. J. O'Brien. He was Reserve again in the following two years, and finally got his due as Champion

Blue Chintz of Annwood, owned by Miss J. Carter and bred by Mrs D. W. J. O'Brien.

in 1983. Blue Chintz (Chips to his many friends), a dapple-grey gelding, was a very versatile and accomplished pony, winner of many performance awards both under saddle and in harness.

A more recent RDA competition is the Hill Samuel Drive to Music, held annually at Windsor. RDA groups can enter as many turn-outs as they like, but each one must have a disabled driver. It is a fancy-dress competition, with a new theme each year. Marks are given for pictorial effect, use of music, and ability of driver and pony. Once again Shetland ponies have shown their aptitude and adaptability. In 1991 the Diptford RDA group won with their single turn-out 'The Grand Old Duke of York'. Robin's Brae Irvine was the pony, and his owner and trainer Mrs Anne Swinscow reported that he had easily learned to walk and trot in time to the chosen music.

5 The ridden Shetland

The Shetland pony has long been admired as a riding pony (see chapter 2). It is not only the Shetland's small size that makes it ideal as a child's first pony, it is the superb temperament and trainability. There can be few more charming sights in the equestrian world than a child happily and confidently mounted on a free-going Shetland pony.

Ridden classes in the show ring

Naturally this attractive sight can often be seen in the show ring. Right from the start of breed shows there have been classes for ridden Shetlands. The 1964 Newbury Racecourse show had two classes, Leading Rein (riders seven and under) and First Ridden (riders eleven and under). Thirty years later this has increased to the point where the Breed Show has a whole section for Ridden Ponies, including everything from Leading Rein to Working Hunter Pony, with a popular Pairs class. Similarly, the regional breed shows, such as the Central Scotland Group, will always have at least three well-filled saddle classes.

Shetland ponies are sometimes thought of as the leading-rein pony *par excellence*,

Riccalton Thunder, bred by Mrs C. Logan and owned by Mrs R. Webb. This picture shows him at his first outing under saddle, going well at just four years old.

A boy's pony? James Stannard on Littlestoke The White Dove at the Performance Show, Malvern 1995.

Miss Victoria Joyce (at the age of eight) mounted side-saddle on Highwood Moonlight.

so it is not surprising that these classes are always full of well-presented and well-behaved animals. But they are equally capable of being as free-moving a first-ridden pony as any child could wish for. (Though it must be admitted that they need proper schooling, probably requiring a lightweight adult with the experience and technique that a child would not have.) It is noticeable that there is a good proportion of boy riders in Shetland classes, in contrast to the 'Child's Ridden Pony' of thoroughbred or Welsh type; could that be because Shetlands, being so down-to-earth and gutsy, are more attractive to boys?

At one time, quite a number of girls were to be seen riding Shetlands side-saddle. At the last of the Newbury Racecourse shows, there were five of them, but since then they have virtually disappeared. It is very difficult now to find a side-saddle that will fit a Shetland (though there must have been hundreds of them made, in the days when all girls rode that way). The Shetland First Lady of side-saddle riding is Victoria Joyce, who has had great success, including winning her age-group prize at the Ladies' Side-Saddle Association National Championships. Perhaps if enough saddles could be found and enough girls taught to ride that way, there could be a separate side-saddle class at the Performance Show. What a beautiful sight it would be.

The Performance Show

The recent increasing attention to Shetlands as performers has led to the foundation of the Annual Performance Show. It started in 1991 as a one-day show, and by its third year had grown to a two-day show at the Great Malvern showground with

Formakin Shoona, ridden by Lizzie Moon, clears an obstacle in the cross-country jumping at the Performance Show 1994. (Photo by Dr D. Bird.)

Bincombe Phoebe (rider Kimberley Hood), bred by Mrs E. House and owned by Mrs R. Webb. Phoebe was Champion Leading Rein pony and overall Champion in the Performance Awards 1994.

more than twenty ridden classes (there are also of course driving classes; see the next chapter). These include all the usual show ring classes, divided up by age-range of riders, plus some more unusual items such as dressage and cross-country jumping. Shetland ponies and their riders like a bit of fun, and there is plenty of that too at the Performance Show, with not only masses of gymkhana events but also the hilarious 'K9–equine express', for teams of pony-and-rider plus dog-and-handler.

In spite of the fun element, the Performance Show is primarily a superb showcase for what the breed can do. The prestige of the pony that comes overall champion of the show is high indeed.

Shetland ponies in competition with other breeds

It is hard to remember that, a generation ago, opportunities for Shetlands to compete against other breeds were confined to appearing in the Leading Rein class alongside flashier-looking creatures of Welsh or even thoroughbred breeding. Shetlands seldom did well, and serious breeders did not usually bother to show their ponies under saddle at all.

The breakthrough for Shetlands in mixed classes happened suddenly in 1977, when Boffin of Transy, a black gelding bred by Dougal Dick and ridden by his daughter Sarah, startled everyone by winning the Mountain and Moorlands Small Breeds Working Hunter Pony championship at the Ponies of Britain Summer Show. Boffin was the only pony to go clear, over a course of jumps up to 3 feet high and with up to 4 feet spread. An anonymous contributor to the Shetland magazine the next year commented: 'Well done Sarah, well done Boffin, well done Dougal – the three of you did more for the good name of Shetlands in twenty-four hours than many of us have done in as many years.'

True words. Nearly twenty years later, the equine world has become accustomed to seeing Shetlands holding their own in mixed company. There are now several prestigious national titles that are competed for by representatives of the different native breeds. The most important of these are the National Pony Society's championships, for Ridden Mountain and Moorland ponies (the Olympia championship), and for Working Hunter Ponies (finals at the Horse of the Year Show at Wembley). Qualifying rounds are held at major shows throughout the country during the summer, including at the Society's Performance Show. The Shetland fraternity can hold their heads up high, with a very creditable record in the finals. Brindle Miranda, a very successful grey mare owned by the Ulverscroft Stud and bred by Mrs M. Sullivan, won the NPS Working Hunter Pony championship in 1994.

Shetland ponies have a particularly good track record in Pony Pairs classes. The first notable victory of this sort came at the Royal Windsor Horse Show in 1989, when Mrs Renwick entered two pairs of ponies who were at the Show for the Grand National. Up against blood ponies of up to 15 hands, the Shetland pairs, one black, one grey, astonishingly came first and second. One of the greys was the redoubtable Brindle Miranda, who was also in the ribbons (with Fordham Misty) when a Shetland pair stood top of the line in the Ponies UK Pairs Championship in 1993.

The Performance Award Scheme

Arguably the most important of all spheres for Shetland pony enthusiasts is the Performance Award Scheme. At one end, the winner of the Nan French Trophy for the best overall performance pony has prestige as high as any pony in the breed, the leading ambassador for Shetlands as useful animals, not toys. At the other end of the

The perfect hunter: Silver of Thorne, ridden by Miss Joanna Turvill. This photograph was taken many years ago, at the time when Silver was the stallion at Mr and Mrs Turvill's Highwood stud, and shows what a wonderful temperament a Shetland stallion has. He can been seen in his retirement on page 4.

scale, the points system means that the humblest scruff of a gelding who does his duty at local shows in the school holidays can win an award, and rightly so. In the Performance Scheme, ponies and riders are registered separately as competitors. Thus, the same pony may compete as a leading-rein pony with a toddler-rider and as an open-class pony with an older child; or one rider may compete on a number of different ponies. Points are given for winning or being placed at affiliated shows, and in the case of non-competitive activities such as Riding for the Disabled or Pony Club points are given for attendance at rallies. Equally, there are awards for the riders themselves, in age-groups under-5, 6-8, 9-10 and 11-14 years old. The ambitious children who ride the Olympia finalists are joined at the annual awards party by kids who are simply having fun at the Pony Club with their Shetlands.

The Performance Scheme has been running in more or less its present form since 1980 (though the Nan French competition which it superseded had been running for many years before that). It now comprises some dozen categories for ponies and four age-group awards for riders (plus one for riders from Scotland). Up until 1993 the Performance Scheme included both ridden and driven activities, with the Nan French Trophy going to the pony with overall best performance, but more recently the driven scheme has been run separately (see next chapter) and the Trophy goes to the champion ridden pony.

The Shetland Grand National

For many of the public, the image of the Shetland pony is provided by the spectacle of the Shetland Grand National. This wonderfully imaginative event has been running since 1982. Its purpose is to raise funds for charity. At the Great Ormond Street Hospital for Sick Children, two intensive-therapy beds have been funded by the

The Grand National: Bincombe Phoebe and Rougette of Woodbury jumping neck-and-neck at Windsor.

Grand National. More recently the money raised has gone to CLIC, the Cancer and Leukaemia in Childhood Trust.

Qualifying rounds are run at various shows around the country during the summer, and are never-failingly popular with the crowds. The ponies race two circuits of the ring (which varies in size from one show to another, but it is always the main ring so quite large), over brush fences about 18 inches high. The race is run as two heats and a final. There is something moving as well as exhilarating in watching these young riders, got up in silks like real jockeys, galloping their hearts out round the ring. The ten successful competitors take part in run-offs at Olympia in December; the late

The sporty side of Shetlands: Boxleaze Carona, ridden by Alice Bird, competing for the Avon Vale team in the Prince Philip Cup, Salisbury, 1993. (Photo by Dr D. Bird.)

Raymond Brookes-Ward was particularly closely associated with this. There are also display races, some of which have taken the young riders and their ponies to Europe.

Because of the breakneck speed at which the ponies race over the jumps, concern has been voiced about the safety of the Grand National. But in fact it is a condition of entry that the pony and rider have completed a year in the Performance Award Scheme, as an indication that they are capable of taking part. And there have been no serious mishaps.

Hunting

Shetland ponies are brave but sensible, and this combination of qualities make them ideal mounts for children in the hunting field. They have been adept at this since their heyday of fashion in Victorian times (see chapter 2), and as long as hunting continues in Britain, Shetlands will still be playing their part with characteristic keenness.

Riding for fun

Never let it be forgotten that the best riding is done just for the fun of it. Lucky the child that has a Shetland pony to ride for that reason alone.

6   The Shetland in harness

Ever since Queen Victoria made them so fashionable, Shetlands have been well favoured as driving ponies. They have style, strength and stamina – the essential qualities for harness work.

When Shetland breeding began in earnest, at the end of the nineteenth century, there were show classes for Shetlands in harness as well as in hand. The Ladies Hope were very keen drivers, and established a great reputation, particularly with their mare Hoplemuroma, a roan standing only 35½ inches. In 1920 she won a trotting handicap for ponies up to 14 hands high, and she was capable of great speeds with an adult in an ordinary gig, being credited with covering four miles in 16 minutes, a speed of 15 miles per hour.

In the show ring, Shetlands were driven to a show waggon, the idea being that these gave the pony a better chance to show its paces than a conventional vehicle

Show waggon: the Duchess of Devonshire driving her miniature pony Floristan, a typical South Park pony down to his flashy white socks.

would. Also in the interests of lightness, only ladies or boys would drive (with unself-conscious class distinction the rules for the International Horse Show of 1920 stated: 'To be driven by ladies or boys under 16 – stable boys barred'). These classes were lively affairs, with the ponies trotting at top speed to the accompaniment of a brass band playing suitable music such as the Post-Horn Gallop or the William Tell Overture.

After the Second World War, things had changed for harness ponies. They had lost their role as an everyday mode of transport: in town there were hardly any horse-drawn vehicles left except the milk-floats, and in the country cars and motorcycles had replaced horses and ponies. In the show ring there were still a few classes for private driving, trade turnouts and hackneys, but on a scale far reduced from prewar days.

Show driving revived

In the early 1960s a few enthusiasts got together to start up Shetland show driving again. The prime movers were Miss Nan French, Lady Joan Gore-Langton and Mrs Shirley Swannack, all of whom had taken part in the Shetland driving classes before the war. By 1963 they had persuaded four of the major shows to put on classes. As in former days, Shetlands were to be driven to show waggons only (or some other very light vehicle), as either singles or pairs, and judging was on performance only.

After a year or two some entries were Shetlands driven to traditional vehicles – rallis, governess cars, etc. – so that the class would be half-way towards a private driving one. Judges and exhibitors were confused as to what was wanted, and support fell away as a result.

In 1968 Mrs Swannack pleaded for a return to the original idea:

> When the sport was revived, . . . it was intended that if possible the classes should be run the same as before the war. That is, most ponies in show waggons or sulkies, although other vehicles could be used, and the class to be judged *entirely* on the performance of the pony. Providing everything was clean and tidy, nobody cared if the harness was old and the vehicle needed painting or the driver a new hat! It was the ponies' condition, movement and general performance that mattered.
>
> Now, no one seems to know what they want. Most of us used show waggons at first and the cry promptly came that 'only fat black stallions in show waggons ever win. No one with a nice little vehicle stands a chance.' So (reluctantly

on my part), most of us searched for nice little vehicles and made endless extra work and expenses for ourselves. Now I have recently heard it said that the standard of turnouts is too high and so it is no use competing. I must say I am quite baffled.

In my opinion, most vehicles used for Shetlands are too big and heavy, making it impossible for the ponies to move freely and give the same sparkling performance that they can be trained to provide in a show waggon or a very light vehicle. Besides, it is all so much more fun and so much fairer if all competitors have similar types of vehicles.

These very sensible words went unheeded. Show waggons disappeared from the ring, and one show after another dropped its Shetlands-only harness class. By the middle of the 1970s the only ones left were at the Newbury Racecourse Shetland show, and at the British Driving Society's annual show at Smith's Lawn.

And yet show driving survived. As part of the general increase in interest in showing in the second half of the 1970s, some Shetland breeders with suitable stallions began to show them in Open Private Driving classes. In spite of some prejudice

The other way to do private driving: a superb traditional turn-out. This is the late Major Maurice Cox driving two home-bred Marshwood geldings in tandem.

against the little ponies, the quality of some of these turnouts was so high that they made an impression. Perhaps the turning-point was when the Staveley family took first prize at the 1977 Royal Show in the Open Pairs class with Lakeland Lightning and Ulverscroft Cameron.

Harness showing in the 1990s

The problem identified by Mrs Swannack has not yet truly been resolved. The core of Shetland driving in the ring is now unequivocally the private driving class. The standard of turnouts is very high, and a competitor will need a long purse to buy one of the restored or replica traditional vehicles. Mrs Swannack's objection that these vehicles are too heavy, and that the ponies would go better in something lighter, is still true.

It will be said that the problem has gone away because now there are separate classes at Shetland shows for ponies driven to exercise vehicles (and at other shows there will be separate rosettes in the open classes). These vehicles fulfil the needs of letting the pony move more freely and of being 'the same for everybody', but there is no doubt at all that the exercise-vehicle classes are the poor relations. No one with a top-class pony would dream of showing it in anything other than a 'proper' vehicle. There is certainly still a case to be made for Shetlands to be shown in show waggons, as hackneys are.

Nonetheless, private driving classes attract a lot of top-class Shetland competitors. The classes at the main breed show and at the regionals always produce a high standard of entries. Shetlands also now compete very successfully with larger animals in open classes.

The British Driving Society

The Annual Show

The BDS Annual Show has always been an important fixture for Shetlands. It was for some time one of the very few places where Shetlands could compete in a Shetland-only class. There are also plenty of other opportunities for them, in classes such as Mountain and Moorland, Governess Car, or Under 13.2 Ride and Drive. Young drivers of Shetlands can also compete for the Junior Whip title. In the classes for multiple turnouts, Shetlands have done well, particularly in tandems. This, by far the most difficult turnout to drive, seems to suit the Shetland ponies' intelligent approach to their work. There is now the Blue Chintz Cup for the Shetland pony winning most points at the BDS show; it is called after Blue Chintz of Annwood, himself a winner at this show and many others.

National Championships

The high point of the calendar for private-driving enthusiasts is the BDS National Championship show, held at Windsor and sponsored by Thimbleby and Shorland (also well known to the Shetland world as the auctioneers of the Reading Sale).

The first Shetland ever to win through to the grand final was Dandy of Denstone, driven by Diane Robinson and owned by Sue Helps, who appeared in the final in

Dandy of Denstone (bred by H. Deakin), owned and driven by Mrs S. Helps, finalist at the British Driving Society National Championships in 1991 and 1992.

1991 and again in 1992. In the latter year Jo Halnan drove Meonwara Marble and Eastlands Slip Anchor as a tandem to come sixth in the final.

FEI driving

Combined driving competitions are held under the rules of the FEI (Federation Equestre Internationale). The phases are: presentation and dressage, cross-country marathon (almost always with water hazard), and cones. Ponies can compete as singles or in pairs, tandems or teams (including unicorns).

Miss Jo Halnan's stylish and successful tandem (*below*). The leader is Eastlands Slip Anchor, bred by Mrs D. Staveley, and the wheeler is Meonwara Marble, bred by Mrs C. Gardner. The same two ponies again (*bottom*), this time working as a pair, Eastlands Slip Anchor on the off side, Meonwara Marble near side. They are taking part in a sponsored drive in Windsor Great Park in 1994, but the water-hazard they have just negotiated is typical of the kind found in FEI competition.

Although Shetlands have of course tremendous aptitude for this kind of competition driving, their small size goes against them. They have to conform to standard vehicle weights, course distances, etc. that are geared to 'average', i.e. much larger, ponies. However, recently the British Horse Society has been running classes for ponies under 11 hands, with correspondingly reduced specifications. Shetlands can now compete effectively against other small ponies, notably Welsh.

The lighter side of driving

For those without the means for private driving or the physical stamina for combined driving, there are now many other ways to enjoy a get-together with other Shetland drivers, perhaps with a bit of competition thrown in.

Mrs Tupper's team. The leaders are Waterfrets Silver Mist and Littlestoke the Silver Queen, and the wheelers are half-brothers Lockinge Edward (bred by Mrs G. Knight) and Stowell Park Archie (bred by The Lady Vestey, Mrs Knight's daughter). The driver is Paul Gregory, with Mrs Tupper as groom.

A typical informal occasion. Mrs M. Handcock leading a picnic drive through the New Forest, with Courtier of Woodbury and Apollo.

The author driving Lockinge Shelley (bred by Mrs G. Knight) to an exercise cart of her own design.

The last word in informality: Beacon Andrew in his farm cart, driven by owner Mrs E. Braithwaite.

One of these events is the Dressage to Music class, often held in conjunction with combined training events. The judging is mostly on performance and only partly on the appearance of the turn-out, and there is no reason why a well-schooled pony in a not-too-special vehicle should not come up with a performance of real elegance and style to win the day.

A more outgoing type of pony might enjoy the scurry competition, the object of which is simply to get round a twisting course in the fastest possible time without knocking off any of the balls. It is a great spectator sport, and the ponies are happy to show off to the crowd. No Shetland show would be complete without a hotly contested scurry, and the scurry is one of the most popular events at the Horse of the Year Show, with Shetlands well to the fore.

But for many people the best thing about driving is rallying, simply meeting up with like-minded people to enjoy a drive in the countryside, share a picnic, and gossip about the ponies. A quintessentially British pastime.

The Shetland Pony Stud-Book Society Driving Scheme

Since 1983 there has been a Driving Awards Scheme, parallel to the one for ridden ponies. At that time there were fifteen ponies enrolled in the Scheme; by 1994 there were forty. The range of activities has enlarged even more than the number of ponies and people involved. There are now eleven sections, covering both competitive and non-competitive activities: there are sections for rallies, RDA work, and charity fund-raising, as well as the show classes for singles, multiples and ride-and-drive. Both ends of the age-range are catered for, with awards for both junior and veteran whips.

7   The Shetland pony in the show ring

Showing is not what it was. Merely to read the results of the few agricultural shows that had classes for Shetlands before the war does not give a picture of what showing was like.

It is now taken for granted that the great shows, the Royal Highland Show and the Royal Agricultural Society of England Show ('the Royal') have their own permanent showgrounds. But it was not always so; these shows used to move from one place to another every year (which seems to have made them more memorable for the people involved; 'I remember the year the Royal was at Oxford', you will hear).

The logistics of getting animals to the shows was entirely different then to what it is now. Livestock was very often sent by train. (The whole country was served with railway lines, and the railways were punctually and professionally run by staff who were used to loads of all kinds, dead and alive.) Most exhibitors would be showing more than one kind of animal; Mr Kerr of Harviestoun was perhaps not so unusual in showing Clydesdales, Hackneys, and Aberdeen Angus and shorthorn cattle as well as Shetland ponies. The ponies would travel to the show in the charge of the head groom or stockman, with the owner making his or her way separately, and thus not knowing of any mishaps that might befall the ponies on their journey.

All the work of showing fell upon the staff. It was their job to get the ponies into show condition by exercising them through the winter (show ponies, especially stallions, were usually kept in); their job to wash and groom them as the day approached, and also their job to present the animal in the show ring.

After the war the scene changed, of course. Staff were not in such plentiful supply, and pony breeders had to do much more of the work themselves. Thus came in the era of the self-drive horsebox, in which the owner would take him- or herself to the showground, there to encamp in the ramshackle temporary stabling for the duration of the show. In those days there was a parade of prizewinners every day throughout the show, so all the exhibitors and ponies had to stay on. It may have been uncomfortable in bad weather, but it was apparently a very sociable occasion.

The beginning of the breed shows

Up until the early 1960s, there were only a few shows with classes for Shetlands. On the one hand were the major agricultural shows – the two Royals, the Bath and West,

74

Mrs M. C. Cox showing her filly Gloss of Marshwood at the Royal Show, 1968.

the East of England, and so on – and on the other were the national shows such the Ponies of Britain Stallion Show (a difficult one for Shetlands and other mountain and moorland ponies, because it was held in March when the ponies were still in winter coat) and Ponies of Britain Summer Show. But at that time there was a big increase in interest in breeding Shetlands (see chapter 3). The time was ripe for enlarging the horizon for show Shetlands.

The first all-Shetland show took place in 1964; organised by Mrs Knight, it was held at Newbury Racecourse. There were ten in-hand classes: yearling colt or filly, two- or three-year-old colt, two- or three-year-old filly, mare, foal, two- or three-year-old filly (coloured), miniature pony (colt, filly or mare), novice, and progeny group. (There were also one driving and two ridden classes.) This range of classes gave every breeder something to go for, and the show was very well supported.

All the old hands look back on the Newbury all-Shetland shows with undisguised nostalgia. Perhaps because the Shetland fraternity was a smaller world, and a more experienced one in horsey matters, the shows of those days had a camaraderie that has now disappeared.

Mrs Knight ran the Newbury Racecourse shows for nine years with great success. The all-Shetland show, still the only one of its kind, became a two-day event in 1970, with twenty-one classes. By 1975 there were nine all-Shetland shows. These included the show at Unst, with nine classes, the first all-Shetland show in the Islands. And Mrs Knight ran a show at her home, Lockinge Manor, that was the forerunner of the Performance Show (not started until 1991); the Lockinge show consisted entirely of riding and driving classes, except for one in-hand class which was specifically for mares and geldings suitable for riding or driving.

More Shetland-only shows began in the early 1980s. They provided important opportunities for ponies other than standard blacks to display their worth, and they continue to be deservedly popular. The usual format is for there to be separate sections for blacks, coloured and miniatures, with the whole range of classes for age-groups and sexes within each section. Shetland-only shows now cover the country pretty well, so that all exhibitors are fairly near to one; they range from the North of Scotland Group's show at Nairn to the Berry Barton Show in Devon. They all include at least two ridden classes, and often a driving class as well.

The Society's own show

Surprisingly, in view of the great interest in in-hand showing at about that time, the Shetland Pony Stud-Book Society did not think to institute its own show until 1982. The first official Breed Show was held on 25 September at Park Hall, Charnock Richard, Lancs, and had twenty-four in-hand classes which attracted some 250 entries (there were also leading rein, first-ridden, and fancy-dress classes, but no driving). The Society's show has been held every year since then, at a different venue each time. It was held in Scotland for the first time in 1985, at Kinross. For the Society's centenary year, 1990, the breed show was a two-day event held at the Royal Highland Show's ground at Ingliston, near Edinburgh.

Shetland showing in the 1990s

A huge increase in the number of classes available to Shetland ponies has occurred over the past twenty years. Whereas in 1974 there were 83 shows with a total of 313

Progeny class: the Woods family's group were winners of the class for three ponies by the same sire, and champion progeny group at the Society's Annual Breed Show 1994. All sired by Wells Ernest, these are Lathom Jemima, Lathom Jubilee and Lathom Jilly.

classes, in 1994 there were 152 shows with just under a thousand classes. Each show tends to have more classes, so that (for example) where previously there would have been a single class for youngstock, i.e. ponies of one, two or three years old, colts and fillies together, now there will typically be three classes: yearlings of both sexes, two- and three-year-old fillies, two- and three-year-old colts. Within this trend to more and more classes there are several important points.

Firstly, the number of classes for miniature ponies has leapt up. In 1974 there were only three shows that held these, with two classes at the Huntingdon Racecourse show and one each at Red Rice and Roby; only a handful of ponies can have been involved, as there were only 26 entries over these four classes, and some ponies must have been entered for more than one. What a change in 1994 – when there were 101 classes for miniatures. (Miniature ponies will be discussed in detail in chapter 8.)

A similar picture emerges for coloured ponies. The same three shows, plus the Newbury Agricultural Society show, held separate classes for coloured ponies in 1974; twenty years later there were 67 such classes, including five specifically for broken-coloured ponies. Classes for coloured ponies are now rather more frequently met with at Scottish shows, which are conversely less likely to have classes for miniatures.

One welcome feature of the expanding showing scene is the arrival of classes for young handlers. In these, children present a pony in the ring, and the judge looks for the best skill in the handler rather than the conformation of the pony. Nonetheless a real show pony will tend to be a better partner for an aspiring exhibitor, so the rules very sensibly state that a child may show a pony other than one belonging to her/him or her/his parents. Young handler classes are held at the Society's own show, at several of the Shetland-only shows, and at a few others, including Turriff, the local show for the Wells stud.

Another very welcome trend is the way geldings are taken seriously for in-hand showing. Although they were eligible at most shows to compete against other young-stock or against mares, they had no classes of their own until recently. There are now twenty shows that have in-hand classes for Shetland geldings, including the Royal Highland. This is tremendously important, because as Shetlands become better known for their prowess in the various performance spheres, customers from outside the breed will want to come and look at ponies to buy and train for performance.

Championships

The curious thing is that the increase in the range and number of show classes has happened over a time when there has not been a comparable increase in the number of Shetland ponies; in fact the number of adult ponies registered during 1994 was lower than in 1974. It follows that there are more prizes to go round, and there is therefore somewhat less prestige in the winning of them. This is particularly the case with championship rosettes: it used to be exceptional for there to be anything other than Champion and Reserve Champion at a show, even where there might be five or six classes on the card. Now there is almost always a Junior Champion and Junior Reserve as well as the overall championship, and at the larger breed shows there may be eight or nine or even more championships, what with section championships (overall and junior) for the black, coloured, and miniature ponies. There is a body of opinion within the Society against this trend.

However, the greatest honours in the breed are still the ones they always were, and

	Royal Highland	Royal	SPSBS Annual Show
1995	Harviestoun Sarnia	Threapwood Vela	Waulkmill MacLaren
1994	Wells Paula	Hose Elan	Arlingtonshoecroft Polly
1993	Wells Rising Tide	Wells Rising Tide	Hose Element
1992	[not panel judge]	Hose Element	Hose Element
1991	Wells Rising Tide	Rosequeen of Transy	Thane of Hutton
1990	Stow Black Velvet	Merry Marion of Netherley	Merry Marion of Netherley (black) Lockinge Patricia (coloured) Firth Tilapia (miniature)
1989	Hose E-Line	Westpark Elaine	Knock Good Luck
1988	Passionate of St Ninian	Monkcastle Oz	Wells Perfecta
1987	Wells Rising Tide	Dewland Victoria	Lockinge Easter
1986	Hose Personality	Merry Marion of Netherley	Christine of Melland
1985	Westpark Elegance	Henrietta of Nashes	Knock Jessamine
1984	Wells Elixia	Lakehead Double Diamond	Bincombe Volunteer
1983	Wells Final Command	Wells Final Command	Blue Mink of Drakelaw
1982	Wells Remarkable	Bincombe Venture	Wells Realization
1981	Hose Vanesto	Dewland Miranda	
1980	Lakehead Ensign	Lakehead Double Brandy	
1979	Wells Evertrue	Lakehead Double Brandy	
1978	Wells Perfection	Wells Vintage	
1977	Wells Vintage	Wells Vintage	
1976	Lakehead Emma	Lakehead Emma	
1975	Wells Manifesto	Wells Vintage	
1974	Wells Perfection	Wells Manifesto	
1973	Wells Erica	Chatsworth Drogo	
1972	Wells Elsa	Lockinge Giles	
1971	Wells Vijay	Wells Vanita	
1970	Wells Vijay	Harviestoun Roma	

Winners of the three main prizes for Shetland ponies

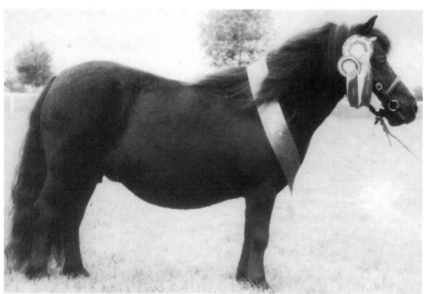

just as highly esteemed and keenly competed for. The premier award for a Shetland pony is the Championship of the Royal Highland Show. This of course was virtually the personal prerogative of the late Mr Harry Sleigh, whose Wells ponies won it on sixteen out of the past twenty-four occasions (see the table).

Only fractionally behind the Royal Highland in prestige comes the Royal, the annual show of the Royal Agricultural Society of England. Again Mr Sleigh has been enormously successful, but here the English breeders have made more impact, with twelve home-bred winners since 1970.

The two Royals will always be the most sought-after prizes, but a rather different and almost as important award is the Supreme Championship of the Breed Show. This show has only been running since 1982 (see above), but it has become established as the venue where the greatest range of top Shetlands can be seen. The two

Champions all: Knock Good Luck (*opposite page, top*) was Supreme Champion at the Society's Annual Breed Show 1989 as a three-year-old filly. She was bred by Mrs D. W. Edwards and owned by Mr and Mrs R. G. Turvill; (*opposite page, bottom*) Wells Perfecta, bred by H. P. Sleigh and owned by Mesdames Pickett and Sargeant, was Supreme Champion at the Society's Annual Breed Show 1988, at the age of fifteen; and (*below*) Mrs Joan Stevenson at home with two of the ponies with which she and her daughter-in-law Mrs Jill Stevenson have had such success. These two ponies, Hose Elan (*left*) and Hose Element, are full sisters and both have been Champion at the Royal Show.

Royals, with no separate classes for coloured ponies or miniatures, have always been the place to see the classic black ponies, the real old Londonderry type, and these are the ponies that always win. No pony other than a black has won either title in living memory, if ever. But the Breed Show is different: the run-off between the champions of the three sections – black, coloured, and miniature – has resulted in a more representative roll-call of Supreme Champions. Over the show's first dozen years the top title has gone to ponies of various colours, including a piebald and a skewbald, and to a miniature pony.

It is worth noting that the only breeders to have shown the champion at all three top shows – the Royal Highland, the Royal, and the Breed Show – are Mesdames J. A. and J. R. Stevenson, who have taken seven such titles, with five different ponies. In fairness it must be said that Wells ponies have also won all three titles, but in the case of the Breed Show they were not exhibited by Mr Sleigh, who chose not to show there.

Competition with other breeds

The top Shetland at a general show always goes on to compete with ponies from the other breeds for the Mountain and Moorland championship. On the whole, Shetlands have not been particularly successful in this; they have such a very different outline from the other breeds that perhaps non-Shetland judges find it hard to compare them fairly. This continues to be the case with in-hand championships even though Shetlands are now coming off better in ridden Mountain and Moorland classes.

8 Miniature Shetlands

A miniature Shetland pony is one that is 34 inches high or less at maturity. That is all. Yet the issue of the miniature ponies is far and away the most controversial one in the Shetland world. It has generated a great deal of debate, some of it acrimonious to the point of being legally actionable. It is no exaggeration to say that the debate is pulling the Shetland fraternity apart, and that it is possible that the outcome will be the loss of the breed as it has traditionally been known.

It has to be said at the outset that ponies of this size have occurred in the breed throughout its history. Some of the early reports of tiny ponies may have been travellers' tales, or perhaps the observers mistook juvenile ponies for adults, but one at least seems well authenticated. Miss Eliza Edmonston, writing in 1856, had encountered small ponies:

> Some of them are very small, from thirty-three to thirty-six inches high; only once have we seen one so diminutive as thirty inches when full grown, and then it could be carried in a person's arms, and became a welcome though singular guest in an English drawing room.

It has been suggested that, in the original state in the Islands, there were not just two basic types of Shetland, the 'Scandinavian' and the 'Oriental' (as described in chapter 1), but a third as well – miniature ponies. This was the view of Ian Sandison, of Houlland, Unst, in a personal communication to the late Maurice Cox. But Major Cox discounted this, feeling that the existence of very small ponies (and other unevennesses of type) was the result of 'lack of care in breeding'. There are several ponies under 34 inches high, both mares and stallions, registered in the first volume of the Stud Book. These include Tom Thumb, the ex-pit-pony who was so important in Lord Londonderry's breeding plans (to keep the size down). It is also true that since the founding of the Stud Book there have been breeders who preferred smaller ponies. Foremost of these were the Ladies Estella and Dorothea Hope, whose South Park stud produced miniature ponies of distinctive style and superb quality. Their stud was carried on by their great-niece the late Lady Joan Gore-Langton.

Show classes for miniature ponies

The idea that a miniature is somehow a separate type of pony dates back to the introduction of separate show classes for small ponies. In the 1960s when in-hand showing was booming, classes with thirty or more ponies forward were usual, and exhibitors of small ponies felt, with some justification, that they did not get a fair share of the prizes. The first Shetland show, held at Newbury Racecourse in 1964 (see chapter 7) introduced the novelty of a class for miniatures. Stallions were excluded, until 1968. The original Newbury class was 'for miniatures, either sex, two years old and over, not to exceed 34 inches at maturity', and there was a trophy, the Gleam Quaich, presented by the Ebony Stud.

Separate classes for the under-34s grew slowly; these ponies were very much a minority interest in the early days. Ten years after the Newbury beginning, there were only four classes, the largest of which had twelve ponies forward (the others had five, five, and four forward). But by 1980 there were twenty classes, with several shows having a youngstock and an adult class for miniatures.

Now, in the mid 1990s, the situation is that there are about one hundred classes for miniature ponies, out of a total number of in-hand show classes of about one thousand. Is this a fair reflection of the numbers of miniature ponies being bred?

Miniatures in the Stud Book

Up until the introduction of a formal height limit for miniature show classes, a small pony was just a small pony. If that was the type they liked, breeders would breed them, but they were not bothered whether their stock matured at 34 inches or 35 or even 36. But after the introduction of the height limit things were different: a 34-inches pony became the target to aim for, and just to be on the safe side breeders aimed for ponies smaller even than that.

This is reflected in the heights of ponies registered in the Stud Book. In 1964, the year that miniature classes began, a very small number of ponies were miniatures. In the Stud Book that year, by far the majority of adult ponies were of standard size, being 37 inches or upwards. The numbers of miniatures were: mares 12 out of 182 (6.5 per cent), stallions and colts 7 out of 88 (8 per cent).

Over the years these figures changed. By the mid 1980s serious fears were voiced that the breed was splitting in half, with a clear divide between standard ponies and miniatures. Certainly in the case of the male ponies the registration figures bore this out. In 1987, 62 were registered, of which 22 (35 per cent) were miniatures. If one includes also the stallions of 35 inches (for these were clearly ponies that had been intended to be under 34 inches but had just overshot the mark), the proportion of miniatures becomes 47 per cent. The impression of the breed falling into two halves is further reinforced by the fact that male ponies of 36 or 37 inches, which were quite numerous in 1964, had virtually disappeared, with only one of each registered in that year. Out of 292 Section A mares registered in 1987, 121 were miniatures (41 per cent). The latest Stud Book available is Volume 94, for 1993. This time it is the mares who show more of a tendency towards two types: the total is 683 mares, with 320 miniatures (47 per cent). The two most 'fashionable' heights are 34 inches, with 87 ponies, and 38 inches, with 88 ponies at that height. In between is a dip, with considerably fewer middle-sized mares being registered than was the case a few years earlier. Most worrying of all is the large number of very small mares. The smallest mares registered in 1964 were 30 inches, but now such small mares are commonplace. The smallest mares now are 28 inches and there were fifty mares of 30 inches or smaller in the latest Stud Book.

The colts and stallions show a slightly more hopeful picture. Out of 89 ponies, 31 are miniatures; this is 35 per cent, exactly the same percentage as in 1987. And the middle-sized stallions have reappeared, with 36- and 37-inch ponies making up a significant part of the year's crop.

Overall, however, there is no escaping the fact that over the past thirty years the breed's average size has changed dramatically. There are far more miniatures, and they are getting smaller.

Damage to the breed?

To look at it another way, the Under-34 class was started in a year when twelve mares and seven male ponies of that size were registered – nineteen ponies in all. Doubtless not all of them were of show quality. It was for the benefit of this mere handful of ponies that this whole exercise began. It is tempting to paraphrase Sir Winston Churchill and to say that 'Never in the field of stock breeding has so much damage been done to so many animals for the sake of so few.' One can only speculate as to what would have happened if the line had been drawn at 36 inches instead of 34, which would have made three times as many ponies eligible in the first place and would have put far less pressure on the breed.

It was not, of course, just the lure of success in the show ring that prompted breeders to go for the miniature ponies. It was more a matter of market forces: it turned out that these ponies were more popular with the customers. If showing was involved at all, and some newcomers to the breed did want to buy ponies to show, these buyers felt that it was easier to choose a pony by criteria that they could understand, particularly by its very small size or its distinctive colouring, than to embark on the esoteric business of knowing which standard black pony was better than which other one. Or, at a more simple level, the new buyers really did not find the black ponies attractive and wanted something easier to relate to. Certainly a large proportion of miniature ponies are coloured: in the latest Stud Book some 80 per cent of the miniature ponies are coloured, and of the coloureds, one in four is a piebald or skewbald. (For standard ponies, coloureds are about 50 per cent, with broken-coloureds again at about one in four.)

The prices now being fetched for miniature stock are out of all recognition for the traditional Shetland trade. At the 1996 Reading Autumn Sale, the top price of 3,000 guineas (which is £3,150 – auctioneers will not relinquish the little trick of operating in guineas so as to get that extra 5 per cent off the punters) was made twice, and there were fifty prices into four figures. These were practically all for miniature ponies. (The only three exceptions were: a top-class Transy mare sold to a Dutch buyer, and two small registered palominos.) Even these prices are by no means the top of the market, as many breeders sell their stock privately. One breeder has regularly achieved five-figure prices for ponies exported to America. There is some evidence that the export trade is the key factor in the high prices of miniature Shetlands. Of the four-figure sales at Reading many were to Dutch buyers; there are always keen buyers from Europe and Scandinavia at the Shetland sales in the UK. Prices at Reading will go higher still if American buyers are present, as they were in 1987 when the top price of 5,000 guineas was paid for a miniature filly foal.

But if the market is there, which it obviously is, and the breeders are willing to supply that market, is there a problem? There is, and to understand why, one has to look at the underlying biology.

The genetic background

To begin with, it is obvious that there are many miniature Shetlands that are of excellent conformation and of absolutely true Shetland type. It is also true that many of these ponies are ridden and driven and that they are just as capable of doing useful work as the larger ponies. But there is also a considerable – and increasing – number of ponies that are *not* of good conformation and *not* of the Shetland type.

The characteristic Shetland was evolved for the particular environment in the Islands. The typical Shetland is that size because of its genetic make-up, and if you want a larger size for some reason, you must cross with a genetically bigger pony. If you want a smaller size, you must breed from ponies that are *genetically* small. A characteristic such as height can be influenced by the environment, of course, but a pony that has been environmentally caused to be small will not pass on its smallness to its offspring. The runt of a litter of piglets or puppies has the same genetic make-up as its larger brothers and sisters but has been stunted by being in a disadvantageous position in the uterus. You could, and would, breed normal-sized offspring from such an animal. Restriction on an animal's growth may also take place after it is born (in fact this is much more usual). A foal that is weaned too early or not adequately fed in its first winter will certainly be smaller than others as a yearling and may never catch up as an adult; but again, the animal is genetically normal and if it is bred from it will have normal-sized offspring. (A typical case of this was recounted to me by a breeder of standard-sized Shetlands. She came across a filly that she had sold as a foal and was horrified by its small size and narrow frame. She bought it back and did what she could to feed it up, but as it was by that time three years old it was not able to catch up much growth, if any. However, put in-foal as a four-year-old it produced the first of many foals that inherited the size their dam would have had if properly reared.) A bout of illness will have the same effect on growth as undernourishment. In these cases, the smallness is acquired from external conditions, and is therefore known as an 'acquired characteristic'. It is an important principle of genetics that acquired characteristics cannot ever be inherited. This was first proved by a German contemporary of Darwin's, August Weismann, and has been continually confirmed in scientific experiments. Thus a pony genetically normal-sized but made small through environmental conditions (as in the example above) will be useless for breeding small ponies: it will breed to the size dictated by its genes, not the size its body happens to be.

Defective ponies

A different situation is presented by a pony whose genes for height are normal but who has a gene (or genes) causing some other defect. This might very well be a defect of the metabolism, preventing the pony from extracting nourishment from its food properly. Such a pony would not thrive no matter how well it was looked after, and it would end up a small pony. It would also almost certainly end up a bad-looking pony, as it would not have reached the symmetry of growth of a properly matured pony. Animals of this sort should not be used for breeding small stock, because they are small on account of an inherent defect. But the important thing to note is that they *would* pass on their smallness to their offspring, as the cause of their smallness is in their genes, not in the environment.

Neoteny

The science of genetics has not yet progressed to the point where the individual genes for each characteristic of a complicated animal like a human or a pony can be identified (though they can be for very small organisms such as viruses and bacteria). However, the principles of genetics are well understood in outline, and all the experimental data from laboratory animals hold good when applied to larger animals, including ponies.

One finding is that there is a gene (or more likely a group of genes) that causes the animal to retain some of its juvenile features in adult life, even though it is fully mature. This is called *neoteny* (pronounced nee-OT-eny, to rhyme with botany). This may very well provide the explanation for the reduced size of some small ponies. Growing slowly, they do not get to normal full size before maturity sets in, and they retain in adult life several features of a juvenile pony, for example the rounded forehead, narrow chest and steep pasterns. This certainly seems to fit with the fact that some miniature ponies grow very slowly, and that they show these juvenile characteristics. Breeding from these ponies to get more small ponies will work, because the smallness is caused genetically (by the neoteny gene or genes), not environmentally. Neoteny is not necessarily an unsoundness in itself, because the pony is simply carrying into adult life the characteristics of a normal, sound juvenile pony. But the adult neoteny pony does look notably different from a pony of standard type (see diagram).

An interesting light is thrown on the neoteny type of pony by some research done by the great Austrian zoologist, Konrad Lorenz, founder of the science of animal behaviour. He discovered that whatever type of animal one is considering, humans are more likely to feel affection for the ones that have juvenile features. (This even extends to cartoon characters: Mickey Mouse and Donald Duck are deliberately drawn to look more like babies than like adults of their kind.) Therefore it is only to be expected that neotenous ponies are the most popular with people who are looking for a pony to be a pet.

True-type small ponies

Finally, there are some Shetlands who mature at 34 inches or less who are that size

rounded
forehead

low-set tail

narrow chest

weak
hocks

shallow-through girth

weak
second thigh

upright pastern

narrow foot

flat forehead

high-set tail

broad chest

deep-through
girth

strong
second
thigh

strong hocks

sloping pastern

round foot

Drawing to show the difference between a neotenous pony (*above*) and a true-type miniature (*below*).

89

simply because they have inherited all the genes for small size. There are probably at least six different genes for size, and for a pony to get all of the small ones together is an outside chance if you are breeding at random, but quite a good chance if you are breeding from ponies you already know to have genes for small size. These are the ideal for breeding miniatures, as they have no unsoundness and they do not have the neotenous characteristics to make them look unlike the breed type.

The table (p. 92) sets out these four basic types of small ponies. It can be seen that although the end product is in a sense the same in all cases, that is, an under-34-inch pony, the underlying causes are different. Type 1 is, as already noted, not genetically caused and will therefore not breed small offspring. Type 2 is genetically caused but should not be used for breeding as the pony is in fact defective. Types 3 and 4 are both feasible as stock for breeding small ponies, but they are of quite different genetic make-up, and crossing them together is likely to give unsatisfactory results.

Dwarfing

One gene that is *not* involved in miniature Shetlands is the dwarfing gene. This gene occurs in many species and varieties of animals (including humans); examples are dachshund dogs and dexter cattle. The typical effect of this gene is to shorten the limb bones, especially the cannons, while leaving the rest of the skeleton almost normal.

A true-type miniature Shetland pony: Firth Tilapia, bred by the late Mrs C. Berry. This beautiful pony was Champion Miniature Pony at the Society's Centenary Show 1990, as a yearling.

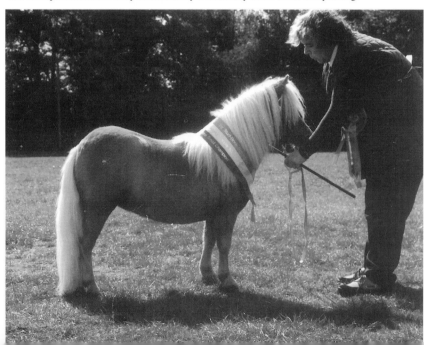

If this gene were involved in the reduced size of miniature ponies, they would be proportionally very short in the legs. That is not, however, what happens; miniatures tend to be if anything longer in the leg than standards, and the reason for this is the neoteny effect described above. To be relatively long-legged is a juvenile feature, and ponies with the neoteny gene(s) will retain it.

Unsound or not

The difficulty comes in deciding whether or not a pony with the neoteny characteristics should be regarded as unsound. All the features that distinguish these ponies are in fact the normal features of juvenile ponies but carried through into adult life. If the features are normal and do not constitute an unsoundness in a juvenile pony, can they be said to amount to unsoundness in an adult? The answer must be yes, because these ponies never get the maturity of limbs that would enable them to work. The reason that one does not ride or drive a two- or three-year-old pony is that its skeleton is not mature; without sufficient bone and without the correct angles of the joints, especially the hocks, the pony does not have enough strength to perform work. The neotenous type of miniature pony remains in this state for the whole of its life. (The miniature pony that is correctly formed (type 4 in the table) is of course as sound and capable of work as any other Shetland.)

Equally, the reason one does not put a two-year-old filly in foal is that she has not the capacity to carry a foal or the growth of pelvis to deliver it safely. In breeding from neotenous female ponies there is a great risk of complications, and these do in fact frequently occur.

What should be done?

Technically, the Shetland Pony Stud-Book Society is perfectly justified in doing nothing. Its formal objective commits it to 'maintaining unimpaired the purity of the breed of Shetland ponies' – and there is no suggestion that the ponies in question are anything other than pure-bred. But what of the next clause: 'promoting the breeding of these ponies'? Surely 'promoting' cannot be taken to mean promoting quantity of ponies bred with no regard whatsoever to quality. What of the breed standard (see Introduction), to which the neotenous miniatures clearly bear no relation? One can only suppose that it is because of the practical difficulties of taking action that the Society's Council has done nothing, in spite of the increasing clamour of calls for them to do so.

Type	Size genes	Cause of pony's smallness	Heritable?
1	normal	undernourishment or illness	no
2	normal	defective metabolic gene	yes
3	normal	neoteny gene(s)	yes
4	small	small size genes	yes

The genetic background to the different types of miniature ponies

The existing structures give little scope for action. In practice, the only control the Society has over the quality of the breed is through the Stallion Assessment Scheme. No male pony may be used for breeding unless he has been licensed, for which he has to pass an inspection at the age of two or over. Refusing licences to colts who show the undesirable neoteny traits would be one way (and at the moment the only way) to eradicate this type of pony.

There are two difficulties. Firstly, a neotenous pony has no characteristics that are not perfectly normal *for a young pony*. How, when you look at him at two years old, do you know whether the colt will grow out of them or not? All colts still have a lot of growing to do between two years and maturity (Shetlands are a slow-growing breed; they are not like bloodstock), and they will all look narrower in the chest and shakier in the joints at two years than they will as adults. It would be hard to tell at two years, but easier at three. A case could be made for automatically deferring the inspection of any colt who is 32 inches or under at two years old.

Secondly, it appears that the problem is not so much with the male ponies. Inspection is already, to that extent, working. The evidence for this is that the most recent registration figures show that only one stallion of 30 inches and three of 31 inches got their papers; none smaller. There has been no trend towards smaller stallions over the past half-dozen years.

The mares, however, do show a very worrying trend towards becoming smaller. The latest registrations show 50 mares of 30 inches or under, plus another 48 at 31 inches. This is where the problem is. In other countries, mares as well as stallions have to be licensed for breeding (see chapter 10). One must accept that the scale of the operation required to inspect mares rules it out at present.

However, there are two ways in which the Society could take action. The first, not very radical and consequently not very effective except as a gesture against the breeding of weedy miniatures, would be to be much more active in ordering foals to be withdrawn from sales held under the Society's auspices. Derek O'Brien, drawing on his many years' experience with Shetlands and with the National Pony Society, suggested this course in a letter to the SPS–BS magazine (1995 edition); he pointed out regulations issued by the Ministry of Agriculture and now ratified by the EC state: 'A foal of any age which is considered immature, weakly, ailing or injured should *not* be presented for sale.' This clause could be used much more rigorously than at present.

The second route is the imposition of a minimum height standard for Shetlands. This is the only thing that will make the difference. A minimum height set at 31 inches would be no problem for the breeders of genuine true-type small ponies, but it would put a stop to the insane race to breed smaller and smaller ponies until they cease to be ponies at all. Mares need not be inspected, but a veterinary surgeon's certificate of height would have to accompany her registration application at the time when she has her first foal. Equally, there would be a minimum height at which foals could be offered at a Society sale, to be strictly enforced.

It is obvious enough that the result of this would be that the breeders of miniatures would split off from the Shetland Pony Stud-Book Society. They already have an interest group, the Group Established for Miniature Shetlands (GEMS), as a nucleus for a new society. The gain for the real Society would be that they were upholding and preserving the true Shetland pony. The loss, however, would be the income from the subscriptions and registration fees from the miniature breeders. This might not be as big a drop as is feared; with only ponies under 31 inches excluded, the 'lost' registrations in the most recent year would be fifty mares (out of a total of nearly 700) and one single stallion. The Society must somehow balance its books to allow this move to be made.

When a pony is not a pony

To some extent, the whole issue of miniature Shetlands is a matter of old worlds versus new. The traditional Shetland breeders have come from the land: whether as members of the aristocracy, or as farmers, or as crofters, they have seen Shetland ponies as one kind of stock among many. These ponies were small enough already, in comparison with beef cattle or hunters or whatever else they might be concerned with. Breeders from that sort of background, horsey to the backbone, are appalled by the ignorance, and hence cruelty, that surrounds too much of the breeding of miniature ponies. Perhaps it is yet one more bad effect of the have-it-all 1980s that ponies are being bred almost as toys – 'My Little Pony' made flesh.

Curiously enough, a close reading of the quote from Eliza Edmonston, who was writing in 1856, shows that she had already put her finger on this very problem. Describing a 30-inch pony, she wrote 'it could be carried in a person's arms, and became . . . a guest in an English drawing-room'.

NO to ponies to be carried about as if they were cats. NO to ponies living in drawing rooms as if they were poodles. The Society must draw the line.

The Shetland Pony Stud-Book Society

The foundation of the Society

The Society was founded in 1890, with commercial rather than altruistic motives. Lord Londonderry and his colleagues had worked hard to establish a type of pony that was the market leader in the coal-mining trade, and they set up a register of breeding stock to keep the breed pure, and to keep it small (see chapter 2).

The first President was the Marquess himself. The committee of twelve reflected the fact that the Society's business was firmly centred on the Islands themselves; recreational breeding might take place elsewhere but breeding for business must be based on Island stock, they believed. This committee consisted of six men resident in the Shetland Islands, four from Scotland, and two from England; one of the latter was Robert Brydon (see chapter 4), who as manager of the Seaham Harbour branch of Lord Londonderry's stud had the closest possible links with the Islands. There were 111 members, most of them crofters. There were also a few founder members who were breeding ponies for their own sake rather than to sell as pit-ponies, and of these by far the most important were the Ladies Estella and Dorothea Hope.

The main concern of the Society was the Stud Book. This was the means by which the type of pony could be controlled, and the threat of unwanted larger stock could be kept at bay. The original criteria for a pony's inclusion in the Stud Book were (a) that it was under 42 inches at maturity and (b) that it had been born in the Shetland Islands, or else was of reputed Shetland origin and had been sired by a pony bred in the Islands.

Oddly, the Society's offices were at Aberdeen, rather than in Lerwick as might have seemed more natural. The Society has always had its base in Scotland, sometimes at the home of the Secretary of the time.

The Society's organisation in the 1990s

Constitution

The Shetland Pony Stud-Book Society in the mid 1990s is a far more professional organisation than ever before. It has been a Company Limited by Guarantee since 1992. This means that the members of Council are Directors, and have formal legal obligations, particularly in respect of the Society's accounts. To be eligible for election to the Council, a candidate must have been a fully paid-up member of the Society for at least five years, and must be under seventy years of age (the latter condition is in accordance with the Companies Act). The eighteen members of Council are allocated by area – the Islands; Scotland and Northern Ireland; England; Wales – and members can only vote in the area in which they live.

The President holds office for two years. He or she is elected as Vice-President by the Council, holds office as Vice-President for two years, and then proceeds to the Presidency. The Past President also sits on Council for two years. This system has the advantage that the top office-holders get every opportunity to learn the business; but the concomitant disadvantage is that changes in the leadership can only be made rather slowly.

Day-to-day responsibilities lie with an Executive Committee, chaired by the President and with two other members of Council. There are six other committees: Stallion Assessment, Judges' Selection, Membership, Public Relations, Artificial Insemination and Embryo Transfer, International. Each of these committees must co-opt two Council members from the Islands for each meeting, regardless of the actual membership of the committee. This is another manifestation of the Society's commitment to its Island roots.

Membership

The membership at the end of 1995 was 1950, made up as follows:

Annual	1273
Annual crofter	13
Junior	136
Life	372
Life crofter	156

This is a slight decrease over the past few years, there having been 2486 in 1992. The decline is partly due to a tightening-up on annual members who were in arrears with their subscriptions. Old life members are dying off faster than new ones are joining.

Staff

The office at Pedigree House in Perth is run by the Secretary and Treasurer of the Society, Mrs Elaine Ward, who came into the post in 1995. She replaced Miss Grace

Crook, who had served since 1992. Miss Crook's professionalism was a revelation to the Society, and she made improvements in its modus operandi in every sphere. The technicalities involved in the negotiations re the European Community (see below) would have been impossible for the Society to manage without her insight and skill. It must be said that prior to Miss Crook's arrival the Society went through the exceedingly unpleasant affair of the conviction of its previous Secretary, Mrs Barbara McDonald, for embezzlement.

The Secretary is supported by one full-time and two part-time members of staff.

The Stud Book

The Stud Book is still the core of the Society's activity. It is published annually, a handsome volume bound in dark red cloth (though its handsomeness is not what it was; the decision in 1988 to typeset the entries in capital letters was regrettable).

The main part of the Stud Book contains the entries for Section A ponies, those with two or more recorded generations on each side of their pedigrees. Then there are the Section B ponies, who are the produce of single-generation mares or mares by B stallions (no B stallions are registered any more; the last ones were in Volume 74).

Stallions

To be eligible for registration as a stallion, a pony must have passed an inspection under the Society's Stallion Inspection Scheme (see below). The fee payable for the inspection also covers the fee for registration in the Stud Book.

The entry in the book gives the pony's name (which must not have changed since he was registered as a foal), his date of birth, colour and height. (If he gets into the book as a two- or three-year-old the height will obviously not be his final height.) His pedigree is given in the form of sire and dam then down the female line to the sixth dam. This enables anyone with a full set of Stud Books (or failing that the very useful indexes compiled by the late Maurice Cox) to reconstruct the entire pedigree for that pony.

Mares

A mare can only be entered in the Stud Book when she has her first foal, which must be by a Section A sire. Up until 1987, the particulars of her first foal were given within the mare's own main entry, but now the foal is elsewhere, listed in the produce section; as there is no cross-reference giving the foal's number this is inconvenient. It also makes it very hard to spot when fillies have been mated at two years old to foal at three, a practice that the Society disapproves of but does not prohibit.

The mare's name must not be changed from what it was when she was a foal. Her date of birth, colour and height are listed. Her pedigree only goes as far down as the granddam on the female line (another change dating from 1987, up till when the pedigree went back to the third dam).

Foals

The foal listing gives the foal's name, sex, date of birth and colour. Its pedigree is just sire, dam and dam's sire. It is now a requirement of the EC that pedigree foals must be registered before 31 December of the year in which they were born, or lose their eligibility; this will impose a hitherto unknown discipline on Shetland breeders to keep up with their paperwork.

A new feature of the foal section is that the foal has a serial number which it will keep for life; previously a foal had no number, but would acquire one on registration as an adult (stallions and mares being numbered in separate series).

Geldings

The register of geldings who were entered as foals gives the pony's name (unchanged since his first registration), and his date of birth, colour and height (if he is fully grown). From January 1996 it has been possible for a foal to be registered straight away as a gelding, so that the same pony need not be registered first as a colt foal and

A gelding reclaimed for the breed by the inspection register: Rastus is without question a pure-bred Shetland, absolutely true to type. Here he is at an RDA session with disabled driver Terry and owner Mrs A. Swinscow.

immediately afterwards as a gelding (i.e. only one registration fee is payable, not two). Proof that the castration was carried out by a qualified vet is required, such proof (letter or invoice) to have the pony's name on it.

Inspected stock

This section lists ponies that have been approved as being of true Shetland type even though their pedigrees are unknown. Most are geldings, but there are also some mares, who are not eligible for registration as breeding mares. These ponies count as registered Shetlands for the purposes of performance work of all kinds.

Stud names

The Society keeps a register (published in the Stud Book) of the names that breeders use to distinguish their own stock. There is no necessity to have such a name, and some of the finest breeders have done without, particularly in the early days of the Stud Book. Stud names seem to have been used hardly at all before 1900, but shortly thereafter a handful of great names come in to the annals of the breed: Mr Mackenzie's Earlshall, Charles Douglas's Auchlochan, and Mrs Houldsworth's Kirkbride, for example.

In order to standardise with the British Central Prefix Register, the Society has regretfully had to limit stud names to prefixes only as from January 1996. Many of the breed's greatest names have been suffixes (Transy and Marshwood to name but two), but these will no longer be allowable.

The exclusive use of a prefix is granted by the Society for a fee of £25, which includes the fee for that name to be entered in the British Central Prefix Register (the Society's Secretary does this). It is of course necessary that the prefix does not already belong to another breeder, either within the Shetland fraternity or among any other breed. The Society now has over 1,400 stud names registered, though not all are in active use. The oldest of them in continuous use is Transy, which first appears in Volume 19 of the Stud Book, and Fairy (Volume 24), which is not the name of a stud as such but was often used by the Ladies Estella and Dorothea Hope for a line of miniature ponies at their South Park stud.

Transfer and Export Certificates

The Society's paperwork is designed to ensure that the whereabouts – or at least the ownership – of all registered Shetlands is known. Foals are first registered under the name of their breeder, who receives a Certificate of Pedigree. If and when the foal is sold, the breeder has to obtain a Transfer Certificate and return the Certificate of Pedigree. The new owner is then sent the Certificate of Pedigree, and if the pony changes hands again the same procedure is followed. Thus if any registered Shetland is sold 'with papers' the Society is aware, and keeps a record of the pony's new ownership. A list of all the Transfer Certificates issued in the year is published in each volume of the Stud Book.

The problem comes when a breeder cannot be bothered to go to the expense of a Transfer Certificate. Although the cost is not huge, the hassle of getting the paperwork done may be too much for breeders at the bottom end of the market. Very many colt foals lose their papers if they are sold away to be gelded; they are lucky if they can eventually be retrieved for the breed via the Inspected Geldings register.

Certificates for ponies being exported are much more watertight, because it is a legal requirement for a pony being taken abroad to have proof of breeding and ownership. This is done by an International Transfer Certificate, which passes via the Society to the corresponding breed society in the country of destination. Again the lists are published in the Stud Book, and they provide interesting information on the fluctuations of the export trade in Shetlands, both in numbers of ponies and their destinations. (Information on prices would be more interesting still.) At £30 for members and £90 for non-members (1995 prices) Inter-Society Transfer Documents are not cheap, but only high-value ponies will be involved. Currently some 200 Shetland ponies per year are exported.

The Society has requested owners of deceased ponies to return the Certificate of Pedigree to the office so that the death of the pony can be noted in the records. (The Certificate is sent back for the owner to keep.) This is an important part of record-keeping for the breed, and even though it cannot be hoped that the coverage will be anywhere near complete, it would be interesting to have a list of 'obituaries' published in the Stud Book.

The Stallion Assessment Scheme

The inspection of stallions is the means whereby the Society can control the overall quality of the breed.

The assessments are carried out by three senior judges from the Society's panel, who assess the pony's action, conformation and trueness to type. Behaviour is also considered, to the extent that a pony who cannot be properly handled and trotted out will automatically fail.

The judges may pass or fail the pony, or they may refer him to the veterinary surgeon. The vet may then either pass or fail the pony, or defer him to be seen again at a later date by the same vet before his pass can be confirmed (this would only happen for a minor veterinary problem, such as a recent knock causing slight lameness).

Colts can be presented for assessment from two years old, though the Society recommends that only exceptionally mature two-year-olds should be put forward. A colt which has been failed by the assessors may be presented again once more, but will not be allowed to try again if the reason for failure was a veterinary problem other than immaturity or an injury or complaint that the vet considered would come right with time.

All colts are blood-typed and given an identification paper showing all markings, whorls etc. Successful ponies have their height recorded by the vet, though if they are less than four years old they will have to be measured again at four by a vet so that the Society has an accurate record of their mature height.

Approximately 60 per cent of colts pass the assessment. Among those who fail, by far the commonest reason is bad action. Lack of Shetland characteristics accounts for about 10 per cent of the failures. As a breed, Shetlands are remarkably free of inherited unsoundness, but nevertheless significant numbers of colts coming forward for assessment have been found to have luxation of the patella.

The annual sales

Another means of controlling the quality of the breed is the Society's role in the annual sales of Shetland ponies. A number of sales are held each year 'under the auspices of the Shetland Pony Stud-Book Society'. What this means is that the Society warrants to the purchaser that each pony is a registered Shetland and that its pedigree is as stated by the vendor. The Society also sends panel judges and a veterinary surgeon to inspect animals on the premises of the sale. They can require that a pony be withdrawn from the sale if it is in an unfit condition or if it shows such bad conformation as to amount to unsoundness. Unfortunately these bans have to be issued more often than should be the case if the breeders themselves were more careful of the welfare of their ponies: at a recent Reading Autumn Sale fifteen ponies failed to pass inspection, out of some 450 ponies presented.

The first official Shetland pony sales were held at Aberdeen, originally thought to be the best venue as it was a compromise between the interests of the vendors based

A view of the Shetland sale held every October by Messrs Thimbleby & Shorland at Reading.

in the Islands and buyers coming from Scotland, England, and further afield. Then in the heyday of the export boom in the 1950s and 1960s the Islanders realised that the world would come as far as their door, and sales in the Islands themselves began, first at Baltasound on Unst and then also at Lerwick. These sales are still keenly attended by foreign buyers wanting the pick of Island stock.

For over a quarter of a century by far the largest sale of Shetlands has been the one held at Reading every October by Messrs Thimbleby & Shorland. Such is the overwhelming dominance of the Reading sale, in terms of prices fetched, that consignments come down nearly every year from the Islands. There has been such an increase in the number of ponies, particularly foals, entered for the Reading sale that the auctioneers have decided to hold another in the spring; the first was held in March 1995.

With the increasing number of Shetlands now being bred, even more Shetland-only sales under the Society's auspices are taking place. There are now sales at Penrith and York. These are convenient for breeders in those areas, but overseas buyers do not attend them, and prices are a fraction of what can be got at Reading.

The average price at the October 1995 Reading Sale was £472, actually a £76 reduction on the year before; the top price was £2625. Earlier the same month, the top price at Baltasound was £210, and at Lerwick £420. The Aberdeen sale achieved good prices, with a stallion selling at £1365, and many mares and fillies making more than £500.

Each sale is preceded by a show, judged by someone from the Society's panel. This show presents a rather droll appearance in comparison with a 'real' show in the summer. For one thing, all the ponies are in their heavy winter coats, looking quite unlike show ponies, and for another, there is a hugely disparate mix of types such as one would never see in the show ring. These classes must be absolute murder to judge; but at least the judge has the consolation of knowing that his or her decision has very little impact on what the pony will fetch on the day. Top prize and top price seldom go together.

The Shetland Islands

One of the Society's main concerns is the welfare of the ponies in their native islands. For many years the Society has run a premium stallion scheme, under which quality stallions are loaned for the season to run on the scattalds. The stallions are chosen to suit the colour and type of the mares on each particular scattald. There are seven scattalds in the scheme: five on Unst, one in Walls, and one in the south Mainland. (There used to be far more scattald grazing on the Islands, but more and more of the open land is being fenced so now the majority of ponies are kept and bred not on the scattalds but in fenced land ('parks') around the crofts.)

There is also a premium filly scheme. This was started in 1983 to encourage breed-

Their native land: Shetland ponies on the scattald, on Unst.

ers to keep back good youngsters for breeding stock. Fillies must be three years old, and they are inspected in the early autumn by two panel judges to make sure they are of a good enough standard. They must be retained for two years and bred from in order for the breeder to keep the premium awarded.

The Judges' Panel

The huge number of show classes requires a correspondingly long list of people officially qualified to judge at shows affiliated to the Society. In 1995 there were just over 100 judges on the Senior Panel. (It might be said that this is a very high proportion of the active membership, who are probably only around 800 in number.) The Judges Selection Committee of the Council lays down guidelines for these judges, as for example the number of shows per year at which they may officiate (not more than six per year, and no two shows to be within forty miles of each other) or the fact that they must not judge a pony that they have bred or sold or had a financial interest in.

The route to becoming a judge is to start as a trainee. This involves judging at affiliated shows alongside a fully qualified judge, who returns a confidential note of the trainee's performance to the Judges Selection Committee. Trainees then attend a session which is in effect a practical examination, and successful candidates become Intermediate Panel Judges. There are about twenty judges on this panel at any one time. They may officiate at shows affiliated to the Society, but not at any of the Society's listed major shows. After five years' service on the Intermediate Panel, judges normally – though not automatically – proceed to the Senior Panel.

Only Senior Panel judges may act as assessors for the Stallion Assessment Scheme, and then only after they have attended at least two assessment days as observers.

Regional groups

One of the liveliest aspects of the Society is the network of local Shetland groups. These began in England in the late 1980s, and by the mid 1990s there were regional groups all over the British Isles. Activities typically include talks on technical matters by experienced Shetland breeders or vets, open days at studs, and coach trips to major events such as the Mountain and Moorland Championship at Olympia. The social aspect of these groups is just as important, with very popular barbecues in summer and Christmas dinners and quiz meetings in winter. The spirit of camaraderie in the regions is a real asset to the breed.

10 Shetland ponies around the world

The first ponies sold from the Shetland Islands to destinations outside the British Isles went to Holland or North Germany. This had probably been going on for as long as the foreign fishing fleets had been coming to the Islands; certainly it is recorded as early as 1633. However, systematic exports did not begin until Victorian times.

The nineteenth century

The earliest shipment of Shetlands exported to set up a stud abroad was probably the one that went to Australia in 1858. Mr Andrew Lyall of Western Australia, acting on behalf of his brother William, bought two stallions and nineteen mares, all of whom made the long journey safely. More shipments were sent soon after, and by the 1870s there were several herds of a hundred ponies or more in Australia. A little later one of the leading enthusiasts was Colonel Thomas Small, who called his estate 'Shetland Heights'; he had many Australian-bred ponies but also bought more stock from the Shetland Islands in the 1890s.

The Americans became very interested in Shetland ponies in the late nineteenth century. The country was booming, and plenty of people had money to spend on fancy livestock from Britain. Dr Elliott of Boston, Massachusetts, a leading equine authority at that time, wrote: 'The Shetland is the most beautiful, the most reliable in disposition, the freest from defect, and the pony that suffers the least from neglect of any known breeds. He is absolutely without the taint of a vicious trait.' Another quotation from America shows an amusing and typical emphasis on value for money: 'If you have a million dollars to spend in giving your child health and happiness, you could not invest it in any way that would accomplish the object better than the investment in a Shetland pony.'

So the Americans bought as many Shetlands as they could. The earliest recorded shipment went to Mr Robert Lilburn of Janesville, Wisconsin, who bought a stallion and some mares from the Londonderry Stud in 1884. Dealers got in on the trade; for instance a Mr Eli Elliot who bought seventy-five ponies in the Islands in 1885 and over one hundred two years later. Prices to the customer were about $150 for a child's pony; that was equivalent to £62 in British money, and if the going rate for a young pony off the Islands was about £15 at that time (see chapter 2), there was plenty of money to be made, especially by setting up studs in America so as to cut out the costs of importing.

In 1888, twenty Shetland breeders met in Chicago and formed the American Shetland Pony Club (it is a matter of pride for this society that it is two years older than the 'parent' society in Scotland). The aims of these breeders were not the same as in Britain. In America, the ponies were bred purely for riding or driving, so there was not the same need to restrict their size; the height limit was set at 46 inches (11.2 hands). Before long Shetlands were being crossed with other breeds to produce a lighter type. Hackneys were used to give a more extravagant action suitable for harness work, and over the years the resulting pony, though still known as a Shetland pony, did not appear to have any native-pony blood at all. The American 'Shetland pony' is a Shetland in name only, and is of no interest or relevance to followers of the real thing.

The true Shetland fared rather better in Canada, another key export market in the late nineteenth and early twentieth centuries. The Douglases wrote:

> In Canada . . . he is in great demand: there he is the school pony; for in the new wheat lands farms are far from schools, and a pony is the child's conveyance. For this purpose a mount is needed which is easily kept, docile, and hardy, and which can be hitched to a fence during school hours without being critical of the state of the thermometer. The Shetland pony supplies the demand, as if he had been created for the purpose.

Canada was the second most important destination for Shetlands, until the First World War put an end to the transatlantic trade.

The first half of the twentieth century

In the first decade of the century, Canada and the USA were overwhelmingly the biggest importers of Shetlands: out of a total of 1399 ponies, 1332 went to America and fifty-four to Canada. Other destinations were various, with Russia (the pre-Revolutionary aristocracy) buying seven ponies, Germany two, and one each to India, South Africa, Austria and Belgium. These all appear to have been sales to personal friends or contacts of the breeders concerned.

Systematic export markets began after the war, though the scale of the trade was much smaller (126 ponies exported in 1920-9, 180 in 1930-9). America was hardly represented at all; the new markets were evenly divided between European countries and far-flung, often tropical, destinations. Shetlands went to India, South Africa, Australia, New Zealand, Argentina and Brazil, and perhaps the most suitable overseas destination of all, the Falkland Islands. In Europe, Holland and the Scandinavian countries made their appearance as buyers. Only top-quality ponies were exported, being bought as foundation stock for studs in their new countries. The home market for Shetlands continued to be depressed (see chapter 3).

After the Second World War, demand from America picked up dramatically, with that country taking more than 50 per cent of the exports until 1960, and at much improved prices. Europe also became a far better market, as postwar economic reconstruction brought prosperity to the sort of people who would want to establish studs of what is essentially a luxury breed. The Netherlands, having bought only thirty ponies in the decade 1950-9, became the most important purchaser from the beginning of the 1970s, taking nearly 50 per cent of ponies exported in the two succeeding decades.

The European Community

By far the most important event in the history of Shetlands abroad has been the impact of Britain's membership of the European Community (EC). The rules of the EC provide that each breed shall be controlled by the country of its origin, so that the Shetland Pony Stud-Book Society is now the official body for Shetlands throughout the EC. Any pony registered with a stud-book in any other EC country will be eligible to be registered in the original Stud Book, provided that it conforms (a) to the parent society's breed standard (b) to the registration procedures in its own country's society.

This ruling came into effect with the commencement of the EC's Single Market, on 1 January 1992. To cope with the many issues involved, the Shetland Pony Stud-Book Society inaugurated the International Shetland Pony Committee. Appropriately, this met for the first time during the celebrations of the Society's centenary, at Edinburgh in 1990. The countries represented are UK (permanent chair), Belgium, Denmark, Finland, France, Germany, Netherlands, Norway, Sweden and Switzerland. (Membership extends to all European countries with an interest in the breed, not just EC countries.)

The breed standard (see Introduction) was agreed on at the first meeting, but much remained to be done to standardise on other issues. By the mid 1990s, discussions still continued on issues such as: method of identification (microchipping preferred), licensing of stallions (widely differing schemes in use in different countries) including veterinary criteria, licensing of mares, certificates of stinting, artificial insemination and embryo transfer.

Good progress is being made, and a token of the International Committee's achievement is the success of the International Shetland Pony Show, first held in Ermelo, the Netherlands, in 1994. There were 413 ponies, representing every member country except Norway. This show is planned to be held every two years. The Committee has also established a panel of international judges, with twenty judges from Britain and five from every other country.

Netherlands

The senior Shetland society outside Britain is without doubt the Dutch one. It was founded in 1937, but there had been Shetlands in the Netherlands for many years before that: Princess Wilhelmina had a team of Shetlands in 1887. The Dutch society also has the distinction of being the largest, in terms of both people and ponies: its membership of over 5,000 is currently registering 4,800 foals, 1,600 mares and over 300 stallions per year.

The Netherlands: Carlos van Heesselt S.1048. This piebald stallion is typical of the large strong broken-coloured pony that is popular for all kind of performance work in the Netherlands. (Photo by Leontien Ruissen.)

The procedures for inspection and registration are incomparably more rigorous than those in Britain. A stallion's licence must be renewed every two years, and depends on the quality of fifteen foals born in that time; a lifetime licence is based on the quality of the progeny and may be granted when the stallion is eight years old, but if his stock is not of sufficient standard by the time he is twelve, he loses his licence permanently. Mares are registered, and certificates of service by the stallion are obligatory. Every foal is inspected and if there is any doubt about its parentage it is blood-tested. In every year there is a letter that must be used for the initial of the foal's name.

There is a system of premiums for both sexes, awarded annually at separate shows for mares and stallions, on the basis of both conformation and quality of progeny. These can be accumulated to lead to various prestigious titles. There are also nationally organised practical examinations to test the animal's temperament and manoeuvrability; these are open to all breeds of horses and ponies, and in the case of Shetlands can be combined with the breeding premiums to achieve even more prestigious titles.

The Netherlands society divides Shetlands into four classes according to adult height: up to 86 cm, 87–92 cm, 93–8 cm, and 99–107 cm. Currently ponies of the smallest class are enjoying the most favour, and the most popular colour is chestnut with flaxen mane and tail. Among the large ponies, there is a fashion for broken colours, so much so that a show has been held exclusively for them.

Denmark

The Danish Shetland Pony Society was founded in 1959, and by the mid 1990s had some 350 members. Since 1972, only ponies imported from Britain or bred in Denmark from ancestry traceable back to British-registered stock have been eligible to be entered in the Stud Book. Both stallions and mares must also go before a qualified judge at the annual selection, and graded as 1, 2A or 2B (the latter two classes only for junior mares). It is a compliment to the 'mother society' that the judge has since 1972 always been from the Shetland Pony Stud-Book Society's own panel. A four-year-old stallion seeking final selection must also pass a test of temperament (he can be driven, ridden, or lunged); and all stallions are blood-typed when accepted for full registration.

Miniature ponies are not in the ascendancy in Denmark as they are elsewhere: only about 10 per cent of registered ponies are under 34 inches. By contrast, 20 per cent are over $37^{1}/_{2}$ inches. The most frequent colour is black (50 per cent), but chestnut,

Denmark: Supreme Champion for 1995 was Albert, a chestnut stallion by Skovlundens Gordon (by Normandykes Firedance) out of Gry. He is of the colour most admired by the Danes.

especially with flaxen mane and tail, is particularly admired, maybe because that is the usual colour of the Jutland horse, one of Denmark's national breeds.

Germany

Germany is perhaps the most problematic of countries for Shetland ponies. They have been popular there for many years, having first been imported from Britain in 1900. Indeed, they are such a popular breed that in German the word 'Pony' is more or less synonymous with a Shetland pony. There is the problem: the breeding has been controlled only by the Society of Pony Breeders (founded 1943), which was not necessarily concerned with keeping the Shetland breed pure.

Now, equine breeding in Germany is nationally organised by region rather than breed, and the same problem is being perpetuated. Because of this regional division, it is difficult to estimate the total numbers of Shetlands in Germany, but it seems that there are fewer now than there were in the 1980s when Shetlands (or should one say Shetland-type) were more than 12 per cent of all equines.

At that time, many unregistered mares were being used for breeding, and there is no doubt that some rather untypical ones were among them. But the Stud Book was closed in 1987, since when breeding stock has had to go through a selection procedure similar to the one in the Netherlands. They must have a pedigree of at least three generations, but many have a far longer history of true Shetland ancestry. The gene pool is now being enlarged by imports of ponies from Britain. This may correct the tendency towards a light, leggy type that was notable among the German entries at the Ermelo international show.

Miniatures are not admired, and the majority of German Shetlands are over $38\frac{1}{2}$ inches. Blacks are thought to be the best colour. There is some disapproval of broken colours, particularly for stallions. Unfortunately spotted ponies are also permissible even though this is a colour not found in true Shetlands, so these ponies would not be eligible for the British Stud Book.

A special feature of the Shetland scene in Germany is that the leading studs have always been the ones kept at zoological gardens. The zoos at Leipzig and Cottbus have the best studs now, and Berlin, Dresden, Rostock and Magdeburg are also good.

Switzerland

As in Germany, there is no specific breed society for Shetlands. They are catered for by a section of the Swiss Pony Association (founded 1957). There are now some 3,000 ponies registered as Shetlands; the Swiss-bred ones are of known origin, being the descendants of stock imported from the 1950s onwards, mostly from Britain, and there are now substantial numbers of newly imported ponies, from Britain and the Netherlands.

Both mares and stallions must be licensed by selection. In the case of a stallion, he is blood-typed; his licence has to be renewed annually, and he must pass a test of ability in harness or under saddle at age three to five.

Finland

The Shetland pony is a newcomer to Finland. The Finnish Shetland Pony Society was founded in 1989, at which time there were 411 mares and twenty-five stallions in the stud book. These were all ponies with known pedigrees, traced back to stock imported from Britain, Sweden and the Netherlands. Indigenous breeding is now gathering momentum, with some 200 foals per year being bred. Both stallions and mares are blood-typed.

France

The French society is called 'Groupement des Eleveurs de Poneys Shetland', and has about 220 members. Procedures follow those of the British Stud-Book Society fairly closely. Thus mares are not licensed, while stallions have a once-for-all inspection and are blood-typed.

Sweden

The Swedish Shetland Pony Society celebrated its twenty-fifth anniversary in 1994, having been founded in 1969. It is one of the largest, with about 1,800 foals registered per year and a total of over 12,000 ponies in the Stud Book. Larger ponies are more favoured, especially a traditional type of black or chestnut.

Australia

No country anywhere has taken the Shetland so much to its heart as Australia. As noted, this was the first country to take a shipment of ponies specifically for founding a stud abroad – and that was in 1858.

The first ponies registered in the Shetland Pony Stud Book to go to Australia were bought by Mrs Maclellan, of 'Shetland Heights', in 1911. In 1912 she imported a stallion bred by the Ladies Hope, named Halcyon of Bodiam. This beautiful pony was the foundation sire of registered Shetlands in Australia. He was joined in the 1920s by stallions of Transy and Penniwells breeding.

The Australian Pony Stud Book was founded in 1931, and included Shetlands in its first volume. This is still the book in which registrations are recorded, but the active support of the breed takes place within the Shetland Pony Owners and Breeders Society of Australia.

Showing is extremely well supported, in spite of the amount of travelling involved for exhibitors. There are up to thirty in-hand classes at each of the six Royal Agricultural Shows (Sydney, Melbourne, Perth, Adelaide, Brisbane and Canberra), plus saddle and harness classes. Ponies are shown in separate classes by height: up to 8.2 hands (34 inches), up to 9.2 hands (38 inches) and up to 10.2 hands (42 inches).

Among the show-quality Shetlands in Australia there are inevitably many blacks, derived from their immaculate Scottish ancestry, but greys are also well to the fore. The famous Fenwick stud, the oldest with a continuous history of breeding in Australia, imported a grey stallion as long ago as 1932.

The larger ponies are favoured, and they are of a type suitable for riding. The market for Shetlands is extremely buoyant, for both breeding stock and riding ponies.

Shetlands in the sun

Shetland ponies have proved amazingly adaptable in making themselves comfortable in hot or even tropical climates. The first records of this go back to the 1890s, when ponies went to India, South Africa and Brazil. South America became a more important destination between the wars, with more than thirty going to Argentina and twenty to Brazil. At that time, too, the first Shetlands went to the West Indies, and to North Africa.

The Middle East saw its first Shetland ponies in the 1950s, and this is now the most important exotic importer of Shetlands, though the numbers involved are very small.

Shetlands do not appear to suffer from the heat. Their only disadvantage in hot climates is that they still grow a 'winter' coat every year, which has to be clipped.

11 Owning a Shetland pony

Where to buy

If you have never had a Shetland pony before, you will perhaps not know where to start looking for one. But you do know what you want it for: a first pony for your child, a driving pony for yourself, possibly several ponies as the foundation of a stud. You will also probably have decided whether you like miniature ponies or standard-sized ones.

Whatever it is that you are looking for, do get advice. Do not be tempted to cut corners by rushing off and buying the first 'adorable Shetland filly' that you see advertised in the local paper (some good ponies do come onto the market in this way, but so do a great many poor ones – beware).

The best way to start is to contact the Shetland Pony Stud-Book Society and get a copy of their magazine. It contains many stud advertisements, most of which are illustrated. Go and see more than one breeder, ideally. Obviously each breeder will try to sell you one of their ponies, but they will also be generous with advice about Shetlands in general, and you are sure to learn a great deal about the breed.

If you want to buy a pony ready schooled for riding or driving, it is as well to ask that the pony should be out at grass when you arrive. Say that you want to see him caught, groomed (including having his feet done), saddled or harnessed and put-to. It is obviously essential that the pony is absolutely quiet for all these procedures, especially if it is to be a child's pony. It is as well, too, to ask to see him loaded into a box or trailer – it would be very annoying to buy the creature and then find that you could not take him home (this has happened).

Buying a pony privately and trying it out thoroughly (maybe even on a week or fortnight's trial) is probably the best thing to do. But some good ponies do come up at the official auctions (see chapter 9), particularly older ponies. If the pony is listed in the catalogue as 'warranted quiet to drive' etc. you are legally protected.

Keeping a Shetland pony

Basically a Shetland pony is an equine like any other, and has the same requirements as any other. However, they do tend to suffer from one or other of two opposite misunderstandings which can lead to them being badly kept. The first is that they are so hardy that they can live on practically nothing; the second is that they are really house pets and are delighted to be fed on titbits. Neither of these is true.

Shetlands are the most attractive and affectionate creatures, and many of them become as attached to their owners as any dog. I have never met anyone who has kept a Shetland who has not admitted to bringing it into the house at one time or another. However, it is one thing to have a pony make occasional visits indoors, and quite another to expect it to behave like a cat or a dog. Perhaps the most important factor is diet: it is extremely important that the Shetland pony lives on its natural diet and does not get filled up with sugar lumps, cucumber sandwiches and bits of chocolate. (Another aspect of this is transport: a Shetland pony, even a tiny one, must travel in a proper box or trailer, and not in the back of a car.)

Grazing

A Shetland pony needs decent grazing. The ideal is to keep them in conditions resembling their native islands, that is on rough pasture where they have to move

Ideal grazing conditions for Shetland ponies: Mrs D. W. Edwards's youngstock on the hills of Cumbria.

around a lot in search of their daily rations. They can be kept successfully in small enclosures, but care must be taken that the pasture does not become 'horse-sick' from over-grazing.

It is of course essential that there is a constant and reliable source of fresh water. Equally essential is a mineral lick.

Shelter

Shetland ponies do not seem to appreciate the benefits of a roofed shelter, and will not go into one even in the wettest and bitterest weather. However, they must have somewhere to go to get out of the prevailing winds. If their field does not already have a wall or thick hedge to provide this, a few yards of hurdle or planked fencing must be put up. It goes without saying that a Shetland does not need a rug.

In summer, they like to have a shady place to stand in (this may be the only time they will condescend to go inside a roofed shelter), and they will gather under a tree or in the shade of a hedge or rock. Artificial shade (hurdles again) should be provided if needed.

Fencing

These ponies are intelligent and inquisitive creatures, and if they are bored they may set about trying to escape to amuse themselves (this is a worse problem with a solitary Shetland than with a herd). The fencing will need to be very secure to keep them

Fencing is important: this post-and-rails fence is fine for horses and larger ponies but is not Shetland-proof. Foals can slip through easily.

in. Perhaps the ideal is a thick, old-established hedge. A wall is good too, though Shetlands are adept at scrambling over the dry-stone kind if it has a low spot. The post-and-rails fence that is so good for larger ponies and horses is *not* Shetland-proof, as foals can pop under the bottom rail in an instant, and even adult ponies can squeeze through unless you put in an extra rail. Barbed-wire fencing, unfortunately very common because it is cheap and effective for cattle, is bad for ponies in general; they can and do get scratched or cut, and they also sometimes rub off their manes; foals can usually get under the bottom wire. Sheep-netting is much better and although it is more expensive it does not have to be tensioned up so thoroughly. Electric fencing is good, too, particularly the mesh sort, and has the advantage that you can move it around to change the run that the ponies have.

Winter feeding

How soon to begin feeding depends on the amount of grass remaining (which varies with the weather each year) and on how heavily stocked your grazing is, but usually the middle of October is about the right time. Shetland ponies seem to prefer meadow

Winter feeding: Mr and Mrs P. J. Tindale's ponies in Staffordshire.

117

hay to the rye mixture sort. It is worth taking the trouble to keep the hay off the ground to minimise waste, but unfortunately the commercially available hay-racks are all too high, so you will have to improvise. Make sure that the ponies can feed well apart, so that they do not kick each other. Shetlands are also fond of root vegetables – swedes, turnips or carrots – which are extremely nourishing and make a welcome change of diet in the winter months. Do not feed any hard food (oats, barley or pony-nuts) to adult ponies: they do not need it unless they are being worked hard every day. As to what constitutes hard work, it is difficult to be specific, because of the range of size of pony, weight of rider, weight of vehicle, type of terrain, etc. For example, an hour's drive for a 42-inch pony in an exercise cart on flat roads is not hard work, but the same session for a 34-inch pony in a traditional vehicle in hilly country definitely is. Even a pony that is doing a day or two a week working is far better off on adequate rations of hay or roots rather than on corn which will make it overheated and hard to manage.

A Shetland pony should never be washed in winter; washing removes the natural grease from the coat so that it is no longer waterproof. If you have to make a Shetland presentable when it is in full winter coat there is nothing for it but just to brush off the mud with a dandy-brush. A well-brushed-through mane and tail make a surprisingly large impact on the pony's general appearance, so concentrate on those! If the pony gets sweated up in the course of his outing, make sure he arrives home cool, and rub him down dry before you turn him out. Shetlands are very tough but it would be asking for trouble to turn out any pony hot and wet.

Shoeing

Shetland ponies have excellent tough feet. No less an authority than the late Glenda Spooner believed that 'here is a breed that can do without shoes if any can'. They *can*, but only if their work is light and is all off the roads. In practice, any pony doing regular work will need to be shod.

Ponies without shoes, particularly youngstock, need to have their feet trimmed every ten or twelve weeks. Your blacksmith will probably grumble about having to do this for Shetlands, because their legs are so short that he will have to stand on his head to reach down to them.

Health

An iron constitution is one of the hallmarks of the Shetland pony, and in general they have extremely little trouble in the way of health. They need the usual inoculations against tetanus, and if the pony is likely to come into contact with others it should have a flu vaccine annually. Worms can be a problem, particularly when Shetlands are kept on intensively grazed land.

The main area of concern for Shetlands is too-rich grazing in spring and summer. They are animals evolved to live on poor pasture, and to make do with a diet varying from scanty in summer to extremely scanty in winter. Rich grass can disagree with them.

Laminitis

The most serious problem is laminitis, inflammation of the soft layer in the wall of the hoof. It cannot be cured, only controlled. If your Shetland shows signs of laminitis, it must have its access to grass severely restricted, and it may even have to spend spring and summer confined to a yard or box.

Fatness

This is not exactly an illness, but it is a bad thing for the pony's general health, fat ponies being more liable to skin trouble and to faulty action which may result in permanent unsoundness. Shetlands are notorious for putting on weight in the summer months. They will often need to be kept off grass for most of the day; and a bit of honest work will do wonders.

Breeding Shetland ponies

If you are intending to buy some ponies to set up a stud, you will have to learn a little about pedigrees. Ideally you will go to some shows (dates are given in the Shetland Pony Stud-Book Society's newsletter) to see which are the sort of ponies you like and to learn which breeding lines they have come from. Then you can go and visit the studs that produce your kind of pony. You are bound to have a wonderful time doing this, as breeders are without exception delighted to show off their ponies and talk about them.

Perhaps you will want to start with a few mares or in-foal fillies; perhaps you will want to buy foals. For the latter, the auction sales can be a very good idea. The pedigrees are given in the catalogue, but your choice will also be influenced by what the foal looks like (bearing in mind that picking a good foal is a highly skilled business).

Some very fine foals indeed can be bought in the autumn sales in the Islands, at prices that are very buyer-friendly (pity the vendors).

Fillies

The best, and 'official' age for first putting the fillies in foal is three (official in that for the show ring a mare with foal at foot must be at least four). However, no less an authority than Maurice Cox has stated that:

> If the fillies are well grown and well developed at two there is no reason why they should not be put to the horse to foal down the following year when they are three.

It should be unthinkable for a filly to be mated as a yearling (even though some of them are sexually mature at that age), but it is now being done. The Society strongly disapproves, and refuses to allow two-year-old mares with foal at foot to be sold at its sales. As from January 1997, the Society will not accept for registration foals born to mares before their third year.

Stallions

It is almost universal practice to run a stallion out with his mares for the summer. Shetland stallions are renowned for their good temper, and there is never a problem with leaving them in charge of mares and foals. They should not be shod at this time (nor should any of the mares); a fair amount of kicking and pawing is part of the normal business, and quite harmless with bare hooves, though potentially dangerous with shoes.

Foaling

Shetland mares seldom have any difficulty in foaling, and it is usually best to leave them alone to get on with it. However, it is important to have the mare somewhere where you can keep a constant watch on her in case something goes wrong. If all goes well, let her deal with matters herself; just watch to make sure that the foal is suckling and that it has passed faeces. Occasionally a foal has to be held to the mare to get it to suckle, or it may have a blocked lower bowel which can be unblocked easily. If the mare is in difficulty with her delivery call the vet. Unskilled intervention

The first few minutes: a mare and her foal can usually manage perfectly well on their own, as these two have done. The mare is Mrs Turvill's Highwood Limelight.

can do more harm than good, and you could kill your mare as well as her foal when both or at least one could have been saved.

Foals

The more foals are handled when they are small the better. They can be halter-broken and trained to lead quietly from the age of three weeks. Do not forget that what is charming behaviour in a little foal is going to be a great deal less charming when the pony is grown up, for example, rubbing its head up and down your leg or putting a front foot up to your waist. It is not fair to encourage these sweet little tricks now when you are going to have to discourage them later on.

Weaning

This is a very stressful time for both mares and foals, and is made infinitely worse if they can hear each other. You may have to resort to borrowing some grazing from a neighbour to get the mares far enough away. All remarks about Shetland-proof fencing apply twice as strongly at weaning time.

There should be no difficulty in getting the foals to eat hard food. The only problem may be arranging things so that the greediest foal does not grab more than its share. The main thing is to put the feed into buckets or some such separate containers that can be spaced far apart. Do not use a single trough that the greedy foal can 'guard' as its own. It is in any case a good thing for you to stay around and watch the foals eating, so that you can spot any early signs of a poor feeder, as well as seeing fair shares between the foals.

Foals are best left outside day and night; provided they have shelter they will not suffer from cold.

Culling

It is far better for your poor-quality foals to be put down at home by your vet than to be taken to market and sold to the meat-man.

Youngstock

Shetland youngstock of either sex need hard food as well as hay throughout their second and third winters, to bring their growth and maturation on. They, as foals, do not need to be brought in at night.

Even if you never intend to use the pony for anything other than breeding, it should learn the following: to be led, to stand tied up, to have its feet picked up and trimmed, and to be groomed all over.

Breaking and schooling

But ideally most Shetlands will go on to do some work. They must be properly broken in and schooled. The reputation they have sometimes had for being tricky is entirely the result of their owners' idleness in assuming that such clever ponies do not need any training. Even the Douglases fall into this error:

> Breaking is usually no difficult matter. A couple of lessons in leading, three in reins, and three in the shafts, with probably one severe conflict of wills in the whole process, will generally break a Shetland pony.

It is not in the least necessary to have 'one severe conflict of wills': a Shetland pony is affectionate and trusting, and its keenness to please you is all you need.

It is natural, but not actually essential for the purpose of training, to want to give the pony a reward if it has been good or has learnt quickly. It is well worth making it an invariable rule that the titbit is only given from a bucket or scoop or bowl; if the pony sees you fishing in your pocket for the sugar-lump or piece of carrot, he will rightly conclude that your pocket is full of these things, and will begin to demand them by nibbling at your coat. This will annoy you, and will be downright frightening to children and non-horsey adults.

Lessons for a Shetland pony who is to be ridden will proceed as for any other riding pony: being led in a headcollar, wearing bridle and bit, wearing saddle, long-reins, backed, ridden away. The small size is an advantage in every phase except the last two. In particular, a Shetland is a nice animal to drive in long reins, because you can see over his head, unlike a full-sized horse that only gives you a view of its tail.

When it comes to backing the Shetland, your problem will be to find a child who is a confident and accomplished rider. Do *not* put up a child who is a beginner. This first rider is there to teach the pony, not the other way round. If you cannot find a good child rider do the job yourself. Do not worry about whether the pony will be up to your weight; it is the bone that makes a weight carrier, and your Shetland can match many a hunter in that respect. Get on yourself, shorten the stirrups as much as you can bear (so as to get your legs against the pony's sides rather than dangling in mid-air), and ride him away.

At a rate of one half-hour lesson a day, it should take about a fortnight to get to backing, and another fortnight for basic schooling afterwards. That is the bare minimum, but even so it is more than most Shetlands get, unfortunately.

Breaking to harness

Shetland ponies have a great talent for harness work. But do take the advice of Mrs Parsons, one of the most experienced Shetland pony whips: before you lay out any money on harness or vehicle, make sure that your pony is suitable, that is, that it is quiet in traffic and will never kick.

It is perfectly possible to break a Shetland pony for harness single-handedly, provided that you have a suitable safe yard in which to do the training. It is possible with Shetlands and not with bigger ponies simply because you can reach everything at once with a Shetland. Shetland stallions are no trouble to break in, and they are perfectly reliable for both driving and riding, even for children.

The following sequence of photographs shows the stages of harness training. The guinea-pig is Mrs Swinscow's Robin (Robin's Brae Irvine), a very well-known driving pony and RDA stalwart, who patiently pretended to be a beginner.

(*Opposite page*)
This sequence of pictures of the breaking in of a Shetland pony to harness features Robin's Brae Irvine and his owner Mrs Anne Swinscow and helpers.

In the first picture (*top*), he is going out for a walk to get used to traffic (note that he is wearing complete harness, including blinkers).

Long-rein work in the yard (*centre*), again wearing full harness.

Learning (*bottom*) to draw a light weight (getting used to the noise is as important as the feeling of pulling).

Wearing sticks (*below*) to get a feel of what shafts will be like.

Putting-to (*above*) for the first time. The driver (*below*) gets in cautiously . . .

. . . but is soon off on a tour of the farm.

The future of the breed

Without question, the Shetland breed faces a difficult time as it comes up to the millennium. There are two threats: first, the miniature ponies, and second, the opening of the Stud Book to EC-registered animals.

As regards the miniature ponies, it appears that there are only two options. The Council of the Stud-Book Society could come to the conclusion that these ponies are distorting the breed, and rule them out by imposing a minimum as well as a maximum height. They would do well to look back at the description in Volume 1 of the Stud Book, which says that the ponies are ideally between 9 and 10 hands. With the current EC situation, setting a minimum height would involve the effort of obtaining the agreement of the rest of the International Shetland Committee. Or Council could

Shetlands step confidently towards the future: the driver's view of Mrs Tupper's unicorn of Silver (Waterfrets Silver Mist), Blue (Littlestoke the Silver Queen) and Willie (Trevassack Willie).

stand by and do nothing. What a grotesque dereliction of duty that would be, when it is publicly acknowledged that half the foals registered as pedigree Shetlands are equine rubbish. Lord Londonderry must be spinning in his grave.

In Europe, there is a substantial worry that back-importation of Continental-bred ponies will bring in genetic elements that are by no means part of the original Shetland inheritance. It is a great pity that the Brussels bureaucrats have set up a framework which is based on the assumption that pony-breeding is a commercial activity. For the vast majority of breeders, and certainly those who have the breed's welfare most closely to heart, this is certainly not the case: Shetlands are a labour of love. It is most definitely not in the best interests of Shetland ponies to let 'market forces' define what is, or is not, a real Shetland.

Spotted ponies are a case in point. They are *not* permissible as Shetlands. Yet for some years now breeders in Britain have been putting registered Shetland mares (especially miniatures, of course) to spotted stallions, for the very simple reason that spotted ponies fetch even more money than the cute tiny Shetlands. These half-bred ponies could be a time-bomb for the integrity of the true Shetland breed.

One of Britain's most experienced breeders points out that the classic Shetland is part of the heritage of the United Kingdom in general and the Shetland Islands in particular. He adds: 'One thing is certain – once a true breed has gone it is gone forever, disappearing into the mists of time.'

Bibliography

Allen, J. R., *Early Christian Monuments of Scotland* (Neill & Co., 1913)

Bedell, L. Frank, *The Shetland Pony*, cited in M. C. Cox, *The Shetland Pony* (A. & C. Black, 1965), p. 34

Benson, J., *British Coalminers in the Nineteenth Century: A Social History* (Gill & MacMillan, 1980)

Bokonyi, S., 'Horses', in J. L. Mason (ed.), *Evolution of Domesticated Animals* (Longman, 1984), pp. 162–73

Brand, J., *A Brief Description of Orkney, Zetland, Pightland-Firth & Caithness* (George Mosman, 1701)

Brooker, M., 'Shetland Island harness', *Shetland Pony Stud-Book Society Magazine* (1982), p. 40

Brydon, R., Introduction to *Shetland Pony Stud Book*, vol. 1 (Shetland Pony Stud-Book Society, 1891)

Campbell, J., *An Exact and Authentic Account of the greatest White Herring Fishery in Scotland carried out yearly in the Island of Zetland by the Dutch only*, repr. from 1750 edn (William Brown, Edinburgh, 1885)

Church, R., *The History of the British Coal Industry* (Clarendon Press, 1986)

Clutton-Brock, J., *Domesticated Animals from Earliest Times* (Heinemann, 1981)

Cossar Ewart, J., 'The making of the Shetland Pony', Appendix to C. and A. Douglas, *The Shetland Pony* (Blackwood, 1913)

Cox, M. C., *The Shetland Pony* (A. & C. Black, 1965)
  'Shetland ponies in harness', *Shetland Pony Stud-Book Society Magazine* (1982), pp. 35–6

Douglas, C. and A., *The Shetland Pony* (Blackwood, 1913)

Edmonston, E., *Sketches and Tales of the Shetland Islands* (Sutherland & Knox, 1856)

Edmonston, L., *New Statistical Account of Shetland 1841* (Blackwood, 1845)

Elliott, S. D., *The Shetland Pony* (Boston, 1906)

Gilbey, Sir Walter, *Ponies Past and Present* (Vinton, 1900)

Gould, S. J., *The Panda's Thumb* (Norton, 1980)

Hamilton, J. R. C., *Excavations at Jarlshof, Shetland* (Ministry of Works, Edinburgh, 1956)

Hibbert, S., *A Description of the Shetland Islands* (Constable, 1822)

Highland Society of Scotland, *Observations on the Islands of Shetland* (1801)

Hjaltalin, J. A. and Goudie G. (transl.) *Orkneyinga Saga* (Edmonston & Douglas, 1873)

Holyoake, J., *Learning to Drive Ponies* (Faber & Faber, 1948)

Ingram, J. and J., 'Unst', in L. Edmonston, *New Statistical Account of Shetland 1841* (Blackwood, 1845), p. 45

Jamieson, C. (ed.), *Hjaltland Miscellany*, vol. 2 (Lerwick, 1937)

Leigh, H., *A General Geographical Description of Zetland* (repr. Scottish Historical Society, 1908)

Lorenz, K., *Studies in Human and Animal Behaviour*, vol. 2 (Methuen, 1971)

Lyon, W. E. (ed.), *Youth in the Saddle* (Collins, 1955)

Mackenzie, R. W. R., 'The Shetland pony', in F. Townend Barton, *Ponies and All About Them* (John Long, 1911), pp. 205–30

Mason, I. L. (ed.), *Evolution of Domesticated Animals* (Longman, 1984)

Meiklejohn, J. J. R., *Introduction to Shetland Pony Stud Book*, vol. 1 (Shetland Pony Stud-Book Society, 1891)

Monteith, R., *A Description of the Islands of Orkney and Shetland in the year 1663* (repr. Thomas G. Stevenson, 1845)

Myers, B., 'The ponies of Shetland Heights', *Shetland Pony Stud-Book Society Magazine* (1980), pp. 45–6

O'Brien, D. W. J., 'Some reflections on the Reading Sales; or Shetland under the hammer', *Shetland Pony Stud-Book Society Magazine* (1995), pp. 38–9

Parsons, E. H., 'Driving Shetland ponies', *Shetland Pony Stud-Book Society Magazine* (1987), pp. 10–13

Patterson, D. M., 'Shetland pony exports 1890–1987', *Shetland Pony Stud-Book Society Magazine* 1988), p. 27

Raeburn, H., *Journal for 1895* (unpubl.), cited in L. S. V. and U. M. Venables, *Birds and Mammals of Shetland* (Oliver & Boyd, 1955), pp. 6–7

Reid Tait, E. S. (ed.), *Hjaltland Miscellany*, vol. 1 (Lerwick, 1934)

(ed.), *Hjaltland Miscellany*, vol. 4 (Lerwick, 1947)

Saunders, G. C., *Your Horse*, 2nd edn (Van Nostrand, 1966)

Scott, Sir Walter, *The Pirate* (Constable, 1822)

Shetland Advertiser (1862)

Shetland Pony Stud Book, vols. 1– (Shetland Pony Stud-Book Society, Aberdeen, 1891–)

Simpson, G. G., *Horses: The Story of the Horse Family* (Oxford University Press, 1951)

Smith, J., *A Description of the Islands of Shetland, &c, by Captain John Smith, who was employed there by the Earle of Pembrock in the year 1633, and stayed a whole Twelve Month there* (repr. Scottish History Society, 1908)

Spooner, G., quoted in W. G. Lyon, *Youth in the Saddle* (Collins, 1955), p. 33

Swannack, S. C., in *Shetland Pony Stud-Book Society Magazine* (Spring 1968), p. 26

Townend Barton, F., *Ponies and All About Them* (John Long, 1911)

Venables, L. S. V. and Venables, U. M., *Birds and Mammals of Shetland* (Oliver & Boyd, 1955)

'Wanderer', 'Ponies at work and play', *The Field* (12 June 1920)

Weismann, A., *Studies in the Theory of Descent*, transl. R. Meldola with Foreword by Charles Darwin, 2 vols. (Sampson Low, 1882)

Wright, W., 'Small draft horses for small holdings', *Shetland Pony Stud-Book Society Magazine* (1979), p. 47

Index

Page numbers in bold refer to illustrations